STOP PLAYING PIOUS GAMES

STOP

PLAYING
PIOUS
GAMES

JO KIMMEL

Abingdon Press
Nashville   New York

Library of Congress Cataloging in Publication Data

KIMMEL, JO, 1931-
Stop playing pious games.
Bibliography: p.
1. Christian life—1960-   I. Title.
BV4501.2.K493   248'.4   73-13625

ISBN 0-687-39595-X

Scripture quotations are from The
Living Bible, copyright © 1971
by Tyndale House Publishers.

MANUFACTURED BY THE PARTHENON PRESS AT
NASHVILLE, TENNESSEE, UNITED STATES OF AMERICA

to the Wednesday morning
prayer group and my church
school class in Phoenix

PREFACE

How grateful I am for all the letters and phone calls and face-to-face encounters I've had about my first book, *Steps to Prayer Power*. I've been hearing such things as, "I really like your easy style of writing," and "It's just as though you're right here, talking with me," and "You'll never know how much your book has helped me," and "I ordered a dozen to give to friends," and "I picked it up one day and read just exactly what I needed right then." Then some of you have said to me, "When are you going to share some more of your ideas with us?" and "What's your next book about?" and "When will your next book be out?" So it's your fault that I'm going to add another

book to the market. The reception you gave the
first book has assured me that you're ready for
some meat in your diet of spiritual food, so get
ready to do some thoughtful chewing on the ideas
I will share with you.

I realize, of course, that no one has a corner on
the truth. Certainly I don't. And as a friend, Tom,
says, "Don't turn me off if I don't use your vocabu-
lary. Keep an open mind and take what I say to
Jesus, and if he and I disagree, you know whom to
believe!" Would you mind rereading this para-
graph? Please don't miss what I said.

What I've chosen to share with you are conclusions I've reached after more than twenty-five-
years experience in a life of prayer. I've stated
my conclusions as chapter titles, and you'll notice
they're in the command form. Obviously, I believe
them to be important.

I hope that I can act as a gadfly to those of you
who may have all the answers down pat or who've
made it all fit neatly in a little box you've labeled
"doctrine," or who've gotten into a spiritual rut
and find yourself going deeper without getting
anywhere. And I pray that those of you who are
eager to grow will find new insight into the life
of the spirit and will use what I give as a spring-
board to plunge into the depths of God.

I'm likely to scold you, shock you, test your

credulity, and challenge you, but I want most of all to encourage you to stop playing pious games and to grow into that maturity to which you're called as sons and daughters of God and as coheirs with Jesus Christ.

CONTENTS

STOP PLAYING
PIOUS GAMES

We all play games with ourselves, with others, and with God. Somehow we hate to admit that there's a lot of the old Adam in us. We want to whitewash ourselves because we hate to admit that not every little thing about us is redeemed. Until we get honest with ourselves and with God we're going to keep on doing what we know we shouldn't do and not doing the things that we should. But when we admit that not all's well with our world, we'll begin to find the power to live life creatively and joyously.

It may be that if you're not playing the particular games I mention in this chapter, you'll get a glimpse of the ones you *are* playing elsewhere in the book. Because even the best of us play games with God.

Tell It Like It Isn't

When I was twenty I wanted to go to Hollywood to break into the movies. In my prayers at that time, I always assured God that I wanted to go to Hollywood only to get into religious movies such as those produced especially for showing in churches. I didn't realize that God read my heart and not just heard my words. Then the day came when I had to tell it like it was, when I had to get honest with God. I was offered a contract with a major studio, and I wanted God's approval. I'd been to college for a year and a half, but it hadn't really challenged me, and I'd prayed that God would open a door for me that would lead to something challenging. When an aunt and uncle in Kansas City, Missouri, told me that they'd take me under their wing if I wanted to go to modeling school, I took that as an open door and went; but jobs came easily, and the challenge went out of it. I asked God to open another door. When a girl from my hometown wanted me to share an apartment with her in Hollywood, I told God that I would go only to get into religious movies, wanting desperately to make good in the big movie industry. Well, I went, and I must say I played the game very well. I followed up every lead I could with the small companies that made religious movies.

But I also followed up leads with major studios, never thinking God knew what I was doing. Then it happened—I was offered a contract with a major studio. The contract would be for a year, and the studio had the option to pick up the contract for the next seven years if it wanted to at the end of the year. I was excited, but I asked to think about it and let the studio know the next week. I knew what my answer would be, but it wouldn't hurt to check it out with the Lord.

Sunday night came and I had a date with a tall, handsome fellow. He, another fellow, my roommate, and I were going out to Long Beach to the amusement park. I was in my dressingroom brushing my hair when I suddenly heard myself saying, "Julie, I think I'll go to church tonight." I looked at myself in the mirror, and I thought, "Did I say that I would go to church tonight?" and Julie said, "Did you say that you're going to church tonight?" and I thought, "Well, I guess I did, and I'd better go." I answered her, "Yes," and I went. There were several young people there to talk with the older youth group. They were from a group called Moral Re-Armament or MRA. They all told how dull life had been until they'd stopped trying to figure out what they were to do and turned their lives over to God. They had then sought his will, got their guidance from him daily, and life be-

came an exciting adventure. As they spoke, it was
as though the wheels that had been going around
inside me, at odds with each other, had suddenly
meshed and began to move together. I knew I
wanted to find God's will for my life. More than
anything else I wanted to do his will.

I asked one of the girls if she'd help me learn
to get guidance, and she said that she would. She
came to the apartment and stayed several days. We
sat down every morning and wrote out the thoughts
that came to us and then checked them with each
other and with the four standards of MRA—abso-
lute honesty, purity, love, and unselfishness. Then
we did what we felt our guidance said to do that
day.

The first morning I got guidance alone I went
into the living room early and sat down with pencil and paper. I began to write out the thoughts
that came into my mind. After a while my pencil
stopped, and I looked to see what I'd written last.
"Go back to college" was written there. That surprised me, and I thought there must be some mis-
take because those words hadn't come into my
mind. I started writing again, and after a while my
pencil stopped a second time, and I saw the words
"go back to college." I realized that I hadn't
thought those words, yet there they were again.
Perhaps God was trying to tell me something. So

I began to talk to him. I told him that I had the opportunity to be a movie star and that I'd be the best one the world had ever known and that I'd show people that you could be a Christian and live in Hollywood and be a part of the movie industry, that I'd make a great deal of money, and that I'd give all but a little to him and his work. I told him I'd be a great witness for him, and when I thought I had convinced him, I started writing again, but it wasn't long until my pencil stopped a third time and the words "go back to college" were there for the third time.

I didn't want to go back to college. I wanted to be a movie star. But I wanted to do God's will, didn't I? I'd tried going my own way and hadn't been challenged and happy. Well, dreams die hard, especially dreams that are just about to come true. I wrestled with my own desires for a long time, but I finally realized that I really wanted to do God's will, whatever it was, and I told him that I'd go back to college. I did go back and took a degree in religion, and I've never regretted it.

Since that experience, I've tried to be honest. Often I pray that God will help me have the courage to examine my desires and motives. Very often he shows me that I'm trying to hide something from him and myself and it's painful for a while, having to see what's in me and admitting it to him. But it clears the air, and then I can get on with living honestly and telling it like it really is.

Don't get me wrong. Often our desires are God's desires. He's given them to us and wants to bring them to fruition with our wholehearted cooperation, but it never hurts to check. Begin now, and be prepared for him to reveal where you're not telling it like it is.

Here Comes the Judge

One of the most tremendous things that can happen to you is to receive the Holy Spirit, to be infused with Jesus. There are many ways this can happen. Some people are literally shaken when Jesus comes to indwell them, some are filled with great joy, others are made very peaceful inside. Sometimes a gift of the Spirit may be received such as prophecy or speaking in tongues or healing. The Holy Spirit comes to you in the way most natural for you to accept him. I tell of my own baptism in the Holy Spirit in *Steps to Prayer Power* and how later I received the gift of tongues. As far as I know there is no set pattern, yet time after time, I'm with people who are convinced that the experience they had is the only valid one for everybody. How we would box God in with our own preferences and convictions. We condemn others because they're going off on a tangent; that is, they don't see eye-to-eye with us. We jump to judgment at the slightest deviation from what we've experienced. Out of sheer self-defense I'm learning that I don't have to see eye-to-eye with anyone else, that it's God's business to correct anyone who needs correcting. A pious, "It's for your own good," just won't cut it. We really are to be non-judgmental, letting love rather than criticism manifest itself through us, for the judgment we give is the judgment we'll get. I don't know about you, but what I want is the judgment of love, and if I'm to receive it, then I must give it; so I'm learning to look for the good in others, especially in those I don't agree with.

I well remember the woman who jumped to the conclusion that I swallow astrology hook, line, and sinker because I carried a key ring with the symbol of Aquarius on it. It was a gift from my daughter Susan, and I treasured it because she'd bought it for me. The woman saw it and asked if I would mind if she prayed for me. I told her I'd be delighted to have her pray for me. For quite some time in her prayer she assured me that she was not condemning me, but then she asked God to lead me out of wickedness, to have me burn all my books, and to bring me back to the true light. She'd jumped to judgment, and I didn't even bother to talk with her about what I believe and don't believe. Her mind was made up about me.

Word Perfect

Some of us have to use certain words to express our faith and belief. No other words will do for us, and when certain words are used in our presence, we equate them with the devil.

I heard a friend tell about listening to a preacher on the radio while driving through Texas. The preacher said, "The King James Version was good enough for Jesus, and it's good enough for me!" Some of us have to have the exact words we grew up with or else we're at a loss, and certainly anyone who uses updated words had better be watched carefully.

I've been amazed at how upset people can get when I mention the word "meditation," which is a perfectly good word as far as I'm concerned, but which apparently conjures up in their minds the mysterious religions of the East. Truly, words can trigger emotions and reactions in us, and I'll have to admit that I've played the game "Word Perfect" quite a lot. For instance, when anyone talked of the "blood of Jesus" all it meant to me was icky-sticky goo. It completely turned me off. Then the Lord did for me what he did for

Peter, that very self-righteous Jew who saw many foods and men as unclean. He gave him a vision, and he gave me one, too, in a Hindu ashram at the foothills of the Himalayas when I was resting on my rope-woven bed one afternoon. I "saw" a beautiful scarlet velvet drape from the ceiling to the floor, and it covered the whole wall. It was the most breathtaking fabric and color I'd ever seen in my life. I marveled at the glory of a piece of cloth and as I marveled, I asked, "Lord, what does this mean?" The answer came from deep within me—"This is my blood; I have covered you with it." My heart leaped up within me, and I said, "Oh, yes, Lord, yes." Since that time the words "the blood of Jesus" have a blessed meaning for me. I'm learning to take words that give me a turned-off feeling and to see what Jesus will reveal to me through them. I've been amazed at what he can reveal when I make myself available to him for his revelation.

I do hope that you'll be free enough in the Lord to allow people to use words which are meaningful to them and, perhaps, even venture out and ask the Lord to reveal to you the deep meaning of some words that turn you off. And don't get upset if someone doesn't understand some of the words and terms you find meaningful and useful. In so far as you can, live at peace with your brother, use

words and terms he's familiar with, love one another, and seek to find your areas of agreement, not
your areas of disagreement. Truth, wherever it is
in you and him, stands alone. It doesn't need anyone's defense. Rather than picking at the doctrine of
another person, look to see if he's bearing the fruit
of the Spirit and especially if he's bearing the fruit
of love. The way to tell a Christian is by his fruit,
not by his words coinciding perfectly with yours.

Now there is one last game I want to share with
you in this chapter, and remember, the ones I've
chosen are only a few that are being played.
They're no worse or no better than any others. They
all block the flow of God's creative love and life.
You'll see other games in subsequent chapters, and
no doubt you'll begin to see some I've not even
mentioned as you get honest with God.

The Hiding Place

I have the tendency to make myself believe I'm
really better than I am. I make a kind of treaty
with myself concerning something, and when I
break that treaty, I try to blame someone or something else. Too often I've tried to blame too many
church meetings or too much doing good for my
snapping at my children or blasting off at some
stupid drivers. After all, I just don't get enough

sleep because I'm running here and there and
doing this good deed and that good deed, and
when I don't get my sleep, I just naturally get
snappish. Then when someone comes in on the
down-to-earth level, I get angry that I'm not allowed to stay in my world of fantasy where all is
ginger-peachy and I'm always the heroine and the
ending always turns out the way I think it should.

Lots of people have been driven away from
God and from the church because of people like
me who play the game of outer piousness by being
at church every time the door opens and by seeking experiences that build the ego, but who in day-
to-day contacts at home, on the road, in stores,
and at work turn into critical, angry, sarcastic,
money-grabbing, unbearable men and women.

God's been showing me that rather than seeking
a hiding place from the reality of the everyday
workaday world and then oozing a false piousness
in it, I'd better make my time with him worth-
while by confessing my inadequacies and turning
to him for his strength—not wallowing in my own
sin but looking to him and accepting his forgiveness and his empowerment. It works. I no longer
have to playact at piousness. I no longer have to
keep a stiff upper lip. I no longer have to paddle
my own canoe or lift myself up by my own boot-
straps. I can simply be me, take me or leave me,

and what a strain has been lifted. Okay, so I stumble and fall; so he's here to help me up and keep me from stumbling again in the same way. What release, what joy, what a great God!

Now, what game are you playing, or should I say games? I'm sure I'm playing some that aren't even named yet, that I'm totally unaware that I'm playing, but I want to know them so that I can stop playing them. I want to know the truth about me so that I can be free. Don't you?

Loving Father, I'm sorry that I've taken refuge in playing pious games, that I've cut myself off from you and others. I want to stop playing cover-up games and really swing into the game of life, using your rules and your power. Show me just what a hypocrite I am, and then flood me with your forgiving love and empower me to live my everyday life with that love flowing through me to others. And, Lord, help me when I see others playing games to refuse to play them with them, but let my refusal be in such a loving way that they'll be wooed to give up their games and get down to the only thing that really matters, letting your love flow through. Amen.

GROW WHERE
YOU'RE PLANTED

I talk with hundreds of men, women, and young people every year about their problems and almost invariably I hear, "If only my husband would get interested in what I'm interested in," and "My wife doesn't seem to understand that I'm tired when I get home," and "I just can't talk to my mom or dad," and "If only I'd have a big experience then I'd know for sure that I have the Holy Spirit," and "My office is hell on earth, and I'm just waiting to retire so that I can do what I want to do," and "If only this depression would lift," and "If only I could stay well. It seems when one thing's cured, something else comes up," and "If only Sam were like my first husband." "If only the minister would preach to my needs." "If only my son . . ." "If only . . ." "If . . ." The game of "If Only" is being played.

Everything would be all right if someone else or something would change. However, as we've shared and prayed together, some of those I've talked with have discovered that they can grow just where they're planted, in the very soil of relationships and situations that they'd complained about before. I'd like to share with you some of the ideas I've shared with them. "If only" you can catch a glimpse of what I'm saying, you'll find a whole, new exciting way in which to live.

Would you believe that it's you rather than anyone or anything else who needs to change? I know it's much easier to say or think it's someone else's fault that you're not as happy and fulfilled as you think you should be, and I know it's easier to spend your time complaining and grumbling than to change your own attitude. I also know that it's easier to feel self-pity that you're in the situation you're in than to do something about it. But as long as you put the blame anywhere but on yourself, you're going to lack the life that's available to you to grow and to produce fruit that will bless yourself and others.

As far as I can make out, we were never promised that life would be a bed of roses with everything going our way. As I remember, we're told that here on earth we'll have many trials and sorrows but to cheer up, for Jesus has overcome the world and to be sure of this one thing, that he'll be with us always, even to the end of the world. So you see, we're told that things won't always go smoothly, but that there is power available to us through Jesus to live abundantly.

There are so many things I like about Paul. He really faced a lot of difficult situations in his life. I especially like what he wrote to the Philippians about his learning to be content whatever the circumstances and his knowing how to live when things were difficult and when they were prosperous and his learning the secret of facing plenty or poverty and his readiness for anything through the strength of Jesus Christ who lived in him.

You know, I could be wallowing in self-pity that I've been left a widow with three daughters to rear. I could be resentful that at the very prime of his life, Ted was killed in a plane crash, leaving me alone with the responsibility of earning a living and providing for a growing family. I could be depressed that there's been no remarriage in the years since his death, that there's been no strong shoulder to lay my head against, and no one to share life's problems and joys on a day in and day out basis. I could be envious of every woman who seems happily married. I could justify taking snatches of happiness with men who either don't want marriage or who themselves are married to other women. I could, if I indulged in the type of egotism which says, "The world revolves around me. I'm to be made happy every minute of every day by everybody and everything." But I've learned, as Paul learned, to be content whatever the circumstances, and I do mean "learned," for it isn't something that's magically happened to me. And if I can learn it, anyone can. But remember that anything you learn well has to be practiced continually in order to be mastered. Then to keep it, you have to continue to practice, especially when you get into a situation where it would be so easy to stop practicing and just allow the situation to go along on its own.

For instance, there's a married man I know whom I don't see very often, but whom I love very deeply. When I do see him we just talk together, sharing ideas and experiences, and then pray together. There's never been the slightest revelation of anything romantic between us, but I've had romantic thoughts and feelings about him. I've wondered what life would be like sharing it with him, and I've wondered what it would be like to be enfolded in his arms. However, I've learned to take my thoughts and emotions and turn them into prayers such as "Thanks, Father, that I'm capable of having deep emotional feelings for another person. Thanks for this man and his wife. Thanks that if I'm ever to know married love again, you'll see to it that I meet the right man at the right time and place."

There've been times when I've been driving along the freeway, and I've really yearned to be with this man, just a sudden unexpected yearning, and I've learned to smile at my emotions and to say to God, "Thanks for him. Thanks that you're blessing and sustaining him right now wherever he is, whatever he's doing. Thanks for blessing his wife and for deepening and strengthening their relationship. Thanks for his children. Thank you, thank you, Father." And then I go right on growing where I'm planted.

You don't have to be driven by emotion. You can harness it and use it to send out blessings to others. You don't have to play the "If Only" game. You can grow right where you're planted, taking every situation and every person in your life and letting the love of God flow through you to them.

I see many men and women who've been awakened to new life in Christ, who become very dynamic and attractive because of the excitement of the joy of the Lord, and I see them drawn to other men or women in their prayer groups or churches.

When your spouse isn't interested or is only half-heartedly interested in the life of the Spirit, it seems a natural thing to think one of the men or one of the women in your group or church is simply marvelous, and you may begin to wish your own spouse were like him or her, or you wish, if you're unmarried, that person were your spouse. You make it a point to sit near the person you admire, and if the group holds hands for prayer you feel a power, a fire, a love flowing from that person. Or you halfway realize there's danger so you sit across the circle, but you let the sparks fly between you, the air crackling with intensity.

Watch it! You're ripe for letting your emotions get the upperhand with you. You have to learn that emotion isn't the gauge to follow. Jesus is, so take your emotions to him to cleanse and use.

After all, you see that person once a week, and you see his or her best foot forward. It would be a different story if you lived with that person day in and day out. There'd be problems with him or her just as there are now with your spouse or with yourself, if you're single.

A woman I know said to me one day, "You seem to be able just to be friends with men. I wish I could. I don't dare be alone with so-and-so because he really turns me on." Well, you can learn to turn off by getting your mind off the person and on to Jesus.

I know it's fascinating to let emotions play around in your mind and body, but that only gives them an opportunity to grow stronger and stronger in you. It's better to say to yourself, "Come on, you, stop the rehearsal. The show's never to get on the road, so cool it," and then begin to thank God for the other person. You can really do it. It's a learned process, and I guarantee that it'll save you and others a lot of heartache and that you'll find in the process that the very life of Jesus flows into and out through you to that person.

My favorite passage of scripture is in John 15 where Jesus talks about his being the vine and our being the branches, and he likens God to a gardener. The gardener mulches, nurtures, waters, feeds, and prunes the plant; and the life in the vine flows into the branches causing them to bear fruit. Most of us are cut off from the vine because we've grown discontented with our circumstances, or we've thought someone else's spot was better, or we've felt that God's pruned us too much, or he's forgotten to give us enough water, or he's let the storms batter us too much. Actually we've stopped letting the vine be the source of our supply.

We've become so concerned about our own wants that we've forgotten to stay attached to the vine. We've wanted to be understood rather than understanding. We've wanted to do our own thing and really haven't known for sure what our thing is, or we've let someone else be our life.

A woman whose husband had been having an affair with another woman said to me in anguish, "Why do these things have to happen? He's been my life." I could only say that these things happen for our growth, for drawing us back to the vine where our eternal life is. I believe with all my heart that we're to center our lives in Jesus, to allow the life in him, the vine, to flow into and through us, the branches. When someone or something else becomes our whole life or our god, that god will eventually crumble. We're to have no other gods before the one God, the father of Jesus Christ and our Father, the gardener who tenderly cares for the vine and the branches. I've learned that when he really is our God, all we need is added unto us at the right time and in the right way.

Now perhaps you've not been able to identify with what I've shared so far. I've chosen to deal with our emotions for the very reason that so many people I talk with are hurting at that particular area of their lives. However, let's get down to what or who is the matter with you. What is it or who is it that you complain about? If you think it would be helpful, take a sheet of paper and make a list of your gripes, bringing into focus the nebulous feelings of unhappiness and resentment that you have. Be specific and be honest. You may resent your very best friend who's able to get away more often than you from the office, or you may be angry with the minister because you don't think he's very cordial with you. Whatever it is, write it down, and don't be surprised if you have a fairly long list, and then again, don't be surprised if you can't put your finger exactly on anything. I've found that people often are not happy, but when we try to find the source of their unhappiness, we can't because the unhappiness really lies with themselves, and they've tried to bury their feelings of inadequacy or lack of education or whatever. Simply put "me" on your sheet of paper.

When your list is made, pray this prayer with me:

Loving Father, here are all the things and people that I think are causing me to be unhappy. I've let them and my unhappiness cut me off from you, the source of all happiness. Forgive me for looking to anyone or anything other than you to meet my needs and bring me fulfillment. Teach me so that I may learn how to connect my life or allow you to graft me back into the vine, Jesus Christ, that I may take my life from him and him alone. Thank you. Amen.

Now you're ready to begin monitoring your thoughts and feelings and words, and when you're aware that you're grumbling about a person or situation or are feeling sorry for yourself, you can stop immediately. And as soon as you stop, try to smile or even laugh at yourself and your reaction, and make a picture in your mind of yourself as a branch, connected to Jesus, the vine, and visualize his life and power and love flowing into you, blessing you and then praise him that he's helping you to grow just where you're planted.

Are you beginning to see that all the elements for growth are around you and in you and that God, the master gardener, knows how to nurture you? He knows just how much sun and rain to give you, just when you need extra food, just how much to stir the soil around you, just when and how to prune. Your business is to let the life in the vine flow through you. Think often during the day about letting the life in the vine flow into and through you. When you get into a difficult situation, picture the vine and the branch and imagine the life flowing into you. A little phrase such as,

"Just you and me, Lord," will remind you, as you say it over and over, that he alone is the source of your supply and that he will enable you to grow where you're planted, bearing in your own daily life the fruit of the spirit, the fruit of love, joy, peace, patience, kindness, generosity, fidelity, tolerance, and self-control.

Loving Father, I really do want to stop fighting people and circumstances that I have to live with. I want to stop playing the "If Only" game. I just let all the fight flow out of me now. Cleanse me completely and then let the life, the abundant life available to me through Jesus Christ, pour into me right now. I'll really try to abide in Jesus, and I'll really try to let you tend and nurture me as you know best. Thanks, Father. Amen.

GET TO KNOW JESUS

Most of us long for someone who totally understands and accepts us, who's a source of strength any time we need help. Some people seek a teacher, a guide, a guru, a husband, a wife, or a friend to rely on. I've been to many different groups, denominations, sects, and religions, but so far I've not found anyone anywhere who comes near having the power and the understanding Jesus Christ has.

Several years ago I planned to go around the world to study prayer and healing, and a friend became very concerned about my going to India to a Hindu ashram. She was afraid I'd be drawn away from Jesus. However, events at the ashram only led me to a deeper understanding of him and his love and to a more total commitment of myself to him.

One day a British woman swami was in my room. She saw the picture of Yogananda and the little vase of flowers and the incense my roommate had on a shelf in the bookcase. She asked her if Yogananda were her guru. Mila replied, "Well, if I could find a living one, I'd rather have him for my guru." The swami smiled and said, "Then he's not your guru, for living or dead he'd be your guru," and I knew beyond any doubt that Jesus is my guru, my teacher, my guide, my redeemer, and my enabler.

Every group I've been to has had something good in it, but time after time after time I've been contacted to help someone whose group or sect or denomination hasn't been able to help, and when I've led the person to Jesus, the help has been immediate and wonderful.

For when you face decisions and crises every day, and I know some of you face them almost every minute, and when you need power, inner power and strength for yourself and others you live with, ideas you've simply discussed or emotional spiritual experiences you've had just won't see you through. What will is a relationship with someone who's wiser and who guides, leads, helps, and sustains. That someone is Jesus Christ.

I literally fell in love with Jesus one Sunday when I read Frank Laubach's book, *You Are My Friends*. I couldn't read the Gospels enough after reading that book because I wanted to know everything I could about Jesus. Frank Laubach had made him so lovable that I longed to know him. I'd known *about* him and I'd played the game of being a Christian for several years, but I didn't know him personally.

Now what's the first thing you do when you meet someone who's interesting? Don't you want to be around that person, find out what he likes and doesn't like, where he's lived, what he does? I have a little saying I purloined from W. C. Fields, "Anyone who loves hot fudge sundaes can't be all bad." When I discover someone I've met likes hot fudge sundaes, my heart warms toward him, and when I find out he also likes to play tennis, I know we'll be friends.

We have an insatiable curiosity to know others. This is good because our curiosity can be directed toward Jesus, and we can get to know him. And even if you've known him for years there are depths that you haven't yet discovered in your relationship with him which can enrich your life. So no matter if you're an old Christian or a new Christian—what I have to share with you can move you into a dimension of living in ever-increasing closeness to Jesus. In the reality of his presence with and in you, you'll find the strength and the wisdom to move through your life and problems with the unshakeable certainty that he loves and cares for you and enables you moment by moment.

I'll never forget the woman who did the most to help the Gospels come alive for me. I was in college when I first saw her. She was leading a retreat for a group of Methodist women of the district, and I slipped into their morning meditations in the dorm lounge.

Genevieve was a lovely woman. The light and love of God radiated from her face. Each morning she read us a brief story from the Gospels and then asked us to close our eyes and imagine we were part of the story. Quietly she set the atmosphere as to where we were, what we wore, how we felt, and what we saw as events unfolded. Each morning it was a tremendously exciting experience, and I began to use her way of reading the Gospels in my own quiet time each day. I grew to know more and more about Jesus as I lived the scenes.

If you've never tried this particular way of reading the Gospels, try it, but don't try more than one story at a time. The Bible isn't to be hurried through so that you can say you've read it a hundred times. Live with it, let the deeper messages it contains speak to you, but most of all, let it get you to Jesus so that you may know him.

Take a short story from a Gospel such as Matthew 15:29–16:1, Mark 9:14-30, Luke 18:35–19:1, or John 8:2-12; read it through twice, then close your eyes and let your inner eye see the scene. Who are you? What are you wearing? What are some of the people around you like? Is it day or night? Is it hot? Is there a cool breeze? Look at the principle characters in the scene. How are they dressed? What do they look like? Build the scene in your imagination until it takes on a life of its own and then hear the conversation and watch what happens.

Someone once told me a story about Frank Baum who wrote *The Wizard of Oz*. As I remember it, Frank Baum came out of his study where he'd been writing; he was irritated and frustrated. When his wife wanted to know what was wrong, he replied in words similar to these, "My characters won't do what I want them to do." His wife sympathized with him, gave him a cup of tea, and he went back to his study. When he emerged later he seemed happy. When his wife asked him what had happened, he said that he'd simply let the characters do what they wanted to do. He'd used his creative imagination to begin with, just as you will to set the scene from the Bible. Then he allowed the story to unfold, just as you will.

As you practice this new way of reading the Bible, I feel sure that you'll receive rich blessings and that you'll wonder how you could have missed hearing about this particular way to read Scripture.

I've talked to many people who really have to discipline themselves to read the Bible. To them it's a duty rather than a delight. But when they put themselves in the scene and experienced the immediacy of Jesus, they could hardly wait for their daily quiet time, and they're discovering that Jesus is in the scenes of their own lives as they unfold moment by moment, day after day. They're learning that as they interact with him, they love him.

A woman I know really turned me off when I first met her, but I had to be associated with her day after day. As I talked with her she began to tell me about herself and her life. She shared deeply with me over a period of months, and I grew to love her dearly. She's a wonderful person, and I know that no matter where I am, if I need someone to pray with me, I can call her, and we can pray together with power. I've often thought that if I hadn't taken time to get acquainted with

her, I'd have missed out on an enriching friendship.

There's another woman I know who was turned
off by me the first time she saw me, but she made a
point of coming over to me, introducing herself,
and sharing ideas with me. I saw quite a lot of her
during the next three days and by the time we
said good-bye, a deep feeling of affection had
grown between us. We keep in touch by sending
each other tapes, usually ending with prayer as we
sign off the "letter." Our friendship has become
a source of strength for us, and it probably
wouldn't have gone beyond the stage of dislike if
she hadn't taken the time to get to know me. It
seems that when we take the time to get acquainted
with someone we usually find ourselves loving that
person.

There's a wealth of information available about
Jesus, not only in the New Testament but in devotional books such as Frank Laubach's *You Are My
Friends* and Leslie Weatherhead's *The Transforming Friendship*. But let reading the Bible, and
especially reading from the Gospels, undergird
whatever else you read. Check what you read in
other books with what you know Jesus said and
did from your reading of the Gospels and from
direct experience with him, and whatever doesn't
square with those, don't waste your time on.

My daughter, Fran, has had some experiences which have sharpened her hunger to read the Bible. One night I was in bed reading when I heard her laughing in her bedroom. I wondered what in the world was so funny. I heard the laugh grow louder as she came upstairs toward my room. By then I was laughing, too, infected by her laughter. She came to the doorway and I said, "What in the world's so funny?" Between chuckles she said, "I was—reading the story of—Jesus—raising Lazarus—from—the dead—and—and—all at once—it hit me—Lazarus—was a—lucky stiff!" Her friendship with Jesus has seemed to enhance every good quality in her, particularly her delightful sense of humor.

To know Jesus, however, there must be more than just knowing about him, as important as that is. There must be a personal relationship with him. A lot of people talk about "the Light," "the Source of all being," "the Christ in you," "Divine Mind," "Christ consciousness," and all sorts of abstract terms when they refer to God. I'm sure that for them the terms are meaningful, and I would in no way denigrate the terms, but I find the word most meaningful to me is "Jesus." As a friend Sabastian Temple has put it in his song, "Jesus Christ is Lord," He is for me, "the visible likeness of the invisible Father." For when I've seen him,

I've seen the Father. My relationship isn't with an abstract idea, no matter how beautiful or blessed that may be. It's with Jesus the person.

I was once talking with a woman who was going through a very disruptive, depressing time. She hadn't much background in churchgoing or Bible-reading. As I spoke to her over a cup of tea about Jesus, she stopped me and said, "Oh, I wish he meant as much to me as he means to you because when you mention his name, your face lights up!"

Believe me, I wasn't always this way. I had to immerse myself in the Gospels. I had to imagine Jesus walked beside me and talked to me, until one day he was there, walking and talking with me, without my having to imagine he was there. Unwittingly I had met the condition Jesus tells about in John 14:21, "and because he loves me, my Father will love him; and I will too, and I will reveal myself to him." I had grown to love him, after falling in love with him through Frank Laubach's book, and he revealed himself to me.

Then the day came which I described in *Steps to Prayer Power* when I received the Holy Spirit and Jesus moved to the inside of me, to become what Paul wrote to the Galatians, "a mighty power within."

Why do we continue to remain powerless and buffeted about in the sea of circumstances of our lives, playing the game of "Christians" but not really knowing Jesus Christ, when there is a mighty power available to us, waiting to come in and help us? John puts it so succinctly in Revelation 3:20, "Look! I have been standing at the door and I am constantly knocking. If anyone hears me calling him and opens the door, I will come in and fellowship with him and he with me."

Jesus is here, right now with you. He promised that he'd be with you always. The problem lies in your inability to see him and to know that he is here. Your inner eye can be opened to see him as you begin to flex the muscles of your imagination by reading the Gospels, story by story as I've suggested, and then by imagining that he's with you in every situation you're in until your awareness of him and your love for him has grown to the point where he can reveal himself to you.

Don't you feel you've dabbled with playing the game of "Christian" long enough, drinking the milk of the spirit by going over and over the fact that you're saved, that a gift or two may be operating in you, that you get the chills when people say certain words that fit with your doctrine, that you've looked long enough for the Antichrist, that you've said all the right words. Beloved, what you need now is not more milk but meat. Drink the milk, indeed, but make your main course the meat so that you may grow just where you're planted into mature sons and daughters of God, the king of heaven and earth, and into joint heirs with Jesus Christ.

Does this sound impossible? It isn't. It's what you've been created for. It's the very thing that the yearning, loving, forgiving God sent his son into the world for, that you might know Jesus Christ and the power which can overcome your world of problems, temptations, worries, fears, and hang-ups. Jesus offers you power to live an abundant life, filled with an inner peace and harmony that the world can't begin to understand and know. Get to know Jesus, yes, through the Bible and through what others write and say about him—and get to know him personally. Live with him in your imagination in every situation in your life, and lo, you'll discover that he's with you always, not only as a power without but as a mighty power within.

Loving Father, help me to learn to know Jesus that I may know you. I believe that he's your ultimate revelation of yourself to me and to the world. How I long to know the peace and the power in my own life that was expressed through him. Teach me, gently and easily, how to move into a deep and satisfying relationship with him. Thank you. Amen.

OVERCOME DISAPPOINTMENT

I'm sure that most of you have been disappointed or let down by people time after time. Every time you've thought, "At last, I've found someone who'll never let me down," he's done something or not done something, said something or not said something you expected him to, and you've been disappointed. Well, you can learn how to overcome disappointment. You can become what I call "unhooked" from people and circumstances so that no matter what happens or doesn't happen you'll be serene, sure of God's guidance, love and care. You can stop playing the game of "Expectation."

Long ago I gave up expecting things of people. I did this because I know myself so well and assume most people are like me, weak and fallible. I need Jesus in the minutest thing I do because I have a penchant for falling flat on my face without him. When I finally gave up expecting things of people and stopped trying to do what I thought people expected of me, I began to depend on Jesus, and I discovered that it really didn't matter what people said and did to me. I became unhooked from people. Now I know beyond a doubt that my happiness doesn't depend on people or circumstances at all, but on my relationship with Jesus.

I don't think I'm a cold, isolated person who's afraid of being hurt and who's shut one door after another on people. I think I lay myself wide open in relationships for people to like or reject, but whatever they do, it doesn't really matter. I've learned to be a God-pleaser rather than a man-pleaser, and I want to share the pivotal experience that unhooked me from setting up standards for other people or from trying to reach standards someone set up for me.

What's more natural than to want to please someone you love? I wanted to please Ted after our marriage, and I must have done a fairly good job of it for about ten years, but then we moved to the island of Madagascar. Before we left the States, we had to visit a psychiatrist and talk with him. One of his questions to me was, "What would you do if something came up that you couldn't share with your husband?" At the time he asked the question I couldn't believe anything would ever come up that I couldn't share with Ted. He was just marvelous with people, listening to their problems and counseling them wisely. I said as much to the psychiatrist, but he persisted. I thought for a while, and then I said, "Well, I'd write a friend in Oklahoma City and ask her to pray for me. She meets with a group of people who believe in the power of prayer, and I'd want her and her group to pray for me." That seemed to satisfy him and off we went to Madagascar. Ted worked as a liaison between the Malagasy Protestant Churches and the National Council of Churches of the United States. He was instrumental in bringing in surplus food and clothing to Madagascar. We moved not only in church circles but also in government ones.

Often we'd be invited to dine with government officials. The diplomatic language of Madagascar is French, and, although I minored in French in college, I read it better than I speak or understand it. Sometimes when I was asked a question, I'd misunderstand it and answer incorrectly. The French and Malagasy didn't mind, but Ted did, and I'd hear about it on the way home. Or someone would tell a funny joke that may not have been just absolutely clean, and I'd laugh, and I'd hear about that on the way home. It became torture for me to go out because I knew that whatever I said or didn't say wouldn't be right, and I'd hear about it on the way home. It seemed that no matter what I did or refrained from doing, it didn't please Ted, and the harder I tried to please him the worse things got. I just kept trying to please him and didn't really know how miserable I was until I began to realize how much time I spent across the street with some friends of ours. These friends simply loved and accepted me as I was. They seemed to enjoy being with me. With them I was relaxed and happy, and then it dawned on me one day that I wished Ted were like the husband of the couple. He seemed so relaxed and easy-going. Why, when he walked, it was like a symphony, and then it struck me—I liked that man better than I liked my own husband. He could start a sentence, and I could finish it. We thought alike; we'd make a wonderful couple, and then wham! it hit me. I seemed overwhelmed with romantic feelings for the man, and I just about died. Here I was a married woman with three children; I was a born-again, Spirit-filled Christian, and I was looking with—what else could I call it but—lust on another woman's husband! What was I to do?

I wrote my friend in Oklahoma City and told her that I needed prayer about my marriage, but as the days went by, no help came. Finally I thought, "Ted's so good with people. He's so understanding. He'll help me," so I told him what I was feeling for the man and I said, "I don't want to feel this way. I love you, and I love the children, and I need you to help me."

I hadn't even thought of what my confession would do to Ted. I hadn't stopped to think how emotionally involved he'd be in the situation or how hurt he'd be to know that he wasn't the only man in my life. Well, he went into shock, literally. He went ice cold, and I had him lie down on the floor, and I covered him with a thick, shaggy rug for warmth. He didn't say a word, and I was petrified by his pallor. When he finally got up, he said in a hard, faraway voice, "You're not a fit mother for my children. You'd better go back to the States and get a divorce," and he walked upstairs to our bedroom, took all his things and moved into the guest room. From then on he didn't talk to me except through the children when we were at home. In public, of course, he acted as though everything were all right. We entertained friends and kept on living a sham life together. I think the thing I remember the clearest of that period of several months of hell was the large picture of Jesus we had over the mantel in the living room. Every time I looked at it, it was a mockery to me. Here we were missionaries, hoping to extend the kingdom of heaven, and we were ourselves living in hell. At least I was. And where was the help I needed to get me out of the situation? What had become of the prayers of my friends back in the States? My own prayers seemed to go as far as the ceiling and then bounce right back at me.

I thought about committing suicide. I looked for the bottle of sleeping pills and couldn't find it. I'd heard that drowning was an easy death, so I could fill the bathtub and drown myself, but what if our daughters found me? There was always the hill called "martyrs hill" that I could drive the car off. But I knew I'd never do that. I knew there had to be a way out of the situation, but what was it?

About this time Ted came into my bedroom one day to talk with me. He began to tell me that on his last trip to Sambava, the vanilla growing area, he'd gone to his motel room. Actually it was a little grass shack, and it was very picturesque. The young Malagasy girl who was cleaning it and making the bed worked with a great deal of love, smoothing the covers tenderly, and it simply went to his heart to see someone work so lovingly. When she told him that she would come back to him that evening to spend the night, he told her to do so. She came back, but he hadn't been able to complete the sex act with her, thinking that if he did he'd betray my trust. Now, he told me, he wished he had.

I think he must have told me in order to hurt me as deeply as I had hurt him, but my heart simply melted, and I felt a great rush of love toward him and I said, "Oh, Ted, I'm so sorry that I haven't been able to satisfy you. I'm so sorry that I haven't been the wife you've wanted me to be. Look, if you want this girl, why don't we bring her to Tananarive and pass her off as the children's maid, and you can have her when you want her?"

I now wonder about the wisdom of my words, but at the time they came unbidden to my lips, and I spoke them without knowing that I was going to say them, and yet as I heard them, I knew I meant them, all of them. At any rate, they shocked Ted. He got a stunned look on his face, and he whirled around and left the room.

He'd expected to hurt me, and I hadn't been hurt. I'd only felt love and sorrow for him. So we were still at an impasse. I cried and cried, asking God to let me know what I was to do, but no answer came and so the days passed.

Then one morning after the girls had gone to school and Ted had gone to the Farm School, I sat down on the bed in my bedroom and got very quiet. I had to hear what God said to me and whatever it was, I would obey. As I sat there waiting,

a peace began to steal into my heart, and I knew
I was to begin packing to return to the States. I'd
find some kind of a job, and although it wouldn't
be easy to leave my three daughters, I knew I'd
be given the strength to do it. Tears of release
flowed as I began to pack, sure that I'd heard God.
Suddenly in the midst of packing, I glanced at
the doorway and there stood Ted. His face which
had been so stony simply crumpled and without
saying a word, we ran to each other and threw
our arms around each other and laughing and
crying we slipped to our knees. When we'd
calmed down a bit, we went downstairs, our arms
around each other and walked outside to sit under
the palm tree and talk. It was the best talk of our
lives. Ted asked me why I never told him what
was wrong with him since he seemed to tell me
all the time what was wrong with me. I said that
I didn't feel that it did any good to tell someone
else what was wrong with him, that it only put
him on the defensive. I told him that I felt that
God would tell a person inwardly what was wrong
and then give him power to change. Besides, what
I thought was wrong with him or someone else
might not be wrong at all but just the way I saw
it. The wrong might really be in me.

He said he was so sorry that he'd made me feel
so inadequate and that if he'd known he was mak-

ing me feel that way he'd have stopped. And let me digress here just a minute, please. Why hadn't I told him how I was feeling? Why didn't he have the sensivity to pick up my unhappiness? I think it was because we'd gotten our eyes off Jesus and had looked to each other for fulfillment. We certainly hadn't communicated our feelings to each other in a healthy way. Well, to get back to what happened now, we decided to go down to the open market and get flowers and bank the fireplace in the living room and have a marriage rededication service that evening. We went to the market and bought bundles of gorgeous flowers and banked the mantel and fireplace. We gave the girls their dinner and put them to bed; then we showered and put on fresh clothes and arm-in-arm descended the stairs to the living room. We slipped off our sandals and knelt before the picture of Jesus above the mantel and there we rededicated ourselves to God and to one another, pledging that we'd let each other grow and be just what God wanted. It was a beautiful, sacred time. The next three months were the happiest period we'd ever known together. A tremendous love seemed to flow out of Ted continually. It was in the way he talked and lived, as though every minute were precious, to be savored for its sweetness. And three months after our reconciliation, he died in a plane crash. How grateful I've been that we had those three months.

It seems to me, in retrospect, that when I'd really given up trying to figure out what I was to do, when I'd become very still and listened to hear what God had to say, that I released my problem so that God could work it out in his own way. My very act of obedience to what I saw as the only solution to our problem, that of returning to the States, opened the way for God to act. I don't know to this day what happened to Ted at the Farm School to make him come back home when he did. I know he'd planned to stay there all day.

I've shared this painful story with you because I know that many of you are either trying to change to please someone, or you're trying to make someone else become what you want him or her to be. As long as things continue as they are, you're going to remain unhappy and disappointed. But isn't it wonderful to know that you need never be disappointed in anyone or anything again, that you can release anyone you're binding and be freed from anyone who's binding you? Part of the good news of Jesus Christ is that he can be trusted to remake in his image anyone you release to him and that he'll do it in his own time and way and do a far better job than you could have done. And then another part of the good news is that all you have to do is please God, and isn't it just great to know that any step you take in his direction to please him is met by his tender, loving acceptance? So all the strain, all the pressure is off. Keep your eyes on Jesus, rather than on yourself or another person, and he'll keep you unhooked from people and circumstances. You'll find that you're able to forgive another person seventy times seven, and you'll find yourself letting people grow at their own rate of speed and not at an unrealistic speed you've set up for them, and you'll discover you've grown relaxed and fulfilled because you're not trying to reach some unrealistic goals someone else has set up for you. You'll be attaining the goals which Jesus empowers you to attain.

Loving Father, I want to stop playing the game of "Expectation" and to be released from the self-imposed hell I'm living in. I release anyone I'm binding to me, and I am released from anyone binding me. I'm going to forgive anyone who's ever hurt me in any way, and I ask to be forgiven for hurting anyone I've hurt. Help me to praise and thank you for working out your perfect will in my life and in the lives of those I love. Help me seek only to please you in all I do and say and am. Somehow, in some way, loose your spirit of freeing love in and through me. Amen.

MAKE LOVE YOUR AIM

I like the phrase "tough love" that I heard one night at a meeting friends took me to at the Hollywood Presbyterian Church. As I listened to the minister talk about tough love and then became a part of a small group which discussed it, I realized I'd been practicing it for several years, particularly with my children. Tough love doesn't express itself in a kind of soupy sentimentality or in a kind of smothering, but does express itself in genuine sentiment and conviction.

After my husband died, my children never wanted me to leave them. Ted had gone away and had never come back, and they were afraid that if I went away, I wouldn't come back either. However I knew that I had to free them from their fear and from their dependency on me, and I also needed to be free to go if I needed to.

I began the process slowly. I'd go to a town some forty miles away and stay overnight at a motel and then drive back home the next day after doing some shopping. It wasn't easy to leave the girls when I knew their fear, but I did leave them, making sure that someone whom they liked stayed with them. I stayed out of town six or seven times over a period of six months. Then I went to a three-day conference in another city. The girls had grown accustomed to my going and returning. From then on, it was easy. I went for a two-weeks television course one summer, and I went on a six-weeks around-the-world trip by myself another summer. I think I missed my daughters more than they missed me.

I could have "loved" them to the point that I'd have stayed with them day after day after day, but somehow God gave me the wisdom to know that that really wasn't love—it was smothering. Much smothering of men, women, and children is passed off as love. It's a game many of us play to feed our egos. I know it's a temptation to believe you're terribly needed by others and that they can't possibly get along without you, but in the long run, you not only smother those others and make them want to flee, and you become smothered in the process.

Looking ahead and trying to see some of the ramifications of actions hasn't been my cup of tea, but I'm learning, and I'm discovering that tough love is needed in everyday living.

For instance, after we moved to Phoenix, Fran often missed the school bus and would come back to the house, and I'd drive her to school. Then one day I realized that as an eighth grader, she should be responsible for getting up and getting to the bus on time. So the day came when she missed the bus, and I said, "All right, I'll take you to school this time, but it's the last time. From now on it's your responsibility to catch the bus and if you miss it, you'll either have to ride your bike or walk."

She did very well for several weeks but then one day she came back to the house after having missed the bus; and she asked me to take her to school. I was doing the breakfast dishes and could have taken her. In fact, I was just drying my hands when I remembered I'd told her I wouldn't take her to school anymore. So I put my hands back into the dishwater and said, "I told you the other day that if you missed the bus you'd have to ride your bike or walk, so why don't you strap your books on your bike and go on?"

"But nobody rides a bike to school," she wailed, "and if I walk I'll be late."

"That's all right. I'll give you a note to explain your tardiness," I said.

"Well, I won't go. I'll just walk over to Westown and wait for the bus to come by at noon," she said defiantly.

"Oh, no, you won't," I replied. "You'll go to school now if I have to drive behind you every inch of the way."

"Then you'll have to," she said and stood looking at me challengingly.

I accepted the challenge, got myself ready, marshalled her out the garage door, climbed into the car, backed out, and started creeping along behind her. As I drove along I carried on a debate in my mind. "It really wouldn't hurt anything if I picked her up and took her to school. I could do it so easily." Then I answered myself, "But you want her to learn to be responsible. If you baby her she'll just depend all that much more on you," and I batted the whole thing back and forth.

I pulled off the road and drove on the berm so that cars could pass me. About six blocks from home, a strap on Fran's sandal broke, and the sandal flapped every time she lifted her foot. I felt just awful. I was a mean mommy making her walk to school with a broken strap on her sandal.

She, of course, was playing the flapping sandal to the hilt. The inner dialogue continued, pity added as well as tears. I suffered because she suffered. Surrepititiously I'd wipe my eyes every once in a while, making sure Fran didn't see me.

Then a thought struck me. So many children were running away from home, what if Fran ran away? What if she just didn't come home after school? What was I doing to my poor child, driving her away from home, turning her into a runaway? The tears flowed faster. Good thing I had on my sunglasses.

A couple of blocks from the school, I pulled ahead of Fran, stopped the car, and called to her that she could ride the rest of the way, brush her hair, and try to fix her sandal. She came rather sullenly to the car and got in. I started toward the school, fighting down a big lump in my throat. Then I had an idea. I said, "Fran, I plan to come by the school this afternoon and pick you girls up. We'll do some shopping and eat dinner out."

"I don't know if I'm coming home or not," she said, and my heart did a turnover, and I blinked back the tears and answered as calmly as I could, "Well, that's something you'll have to decide. I'll be here after school."

By then I'd pulled into the parking lot and stopped. I wrote a note explaining Fran's tardiness, and she got out of the car and started for the school office. Somehow I just couldn't let her go without saying something, and I grabbed the window handle and rolled the window down. "Fran," I yelled, but what was I to say? I couldn't think of a thing. She stopped and turned. I blurted out, "I love you!" My words seemed to hang suspended in the air between us for a long time, and then she smiled and said, "I love you, too," and walked on to the office. What seemed like a great burden rolled off of me, and somehow I knew she'd be there when school was out in the afternoon, and she was.

Many times I've faced situations with my daughters and other people when the easiest thing would have been to let things go unchallenged, but there's been that within me which wouldn't let me take the easy way out, and somehow, then or later, God let me know it was the right thing to do.

I know I fall far short of the loving that's possible, and I'm wanting more and more to be filled with love all the time and to act and react in the loving way. So love, tough love, has become my aim, not to speak with the tongues of men or of angels, or to be able to show off the brilliance of my mind or my extrasensory perception, or to move mountains with my faith or to give up all my worldly goods, or to become a martyr. I just want to be slow to lose patience; I want to be constructive. I don't want to be possessive or to impress others or to think I'm really something. I don't want to insist others do it my way or to take advantage of them. I don't want to be touchy or try to keep score of the wrongs of others. I just want the love of God to be in me and to flow out through me.

Jesus told us we could prove we're his disciples by our love. Apparently our discipleship isn't proved by what we believe but by the fruit we bear. If we bear the fruit of love then we're like God, for God is love, and when we love, we're like him, so John tells us.

Isn't it simple? Love is the answer. But the working out of that love in situations isn't simple, is it? It's enormously complex. It takes all the courage and stick-to-itiveness that we can muster, and it often involves a running dialogue inside us as it did in my experience with Fran, and it can involve tears, too. I wonder if Paul might have had tough love in mind when he suggested that we work out our own salvation?

I want to share with you several things that are helpful to me when I get into a complex situation. I think you will find them helpful, too. A good thing about them is that no one knows you're doing them, for you can carry on conversation and work at the same time these are going on inside of you.

First, relax your jaws. You can do this by feeling a partial yawn in the back of your throat and letting the jaw muscles ease. Then, second, take a long deep breath, and let it go very slowly. Third, take several more long deep breaths, and as you do, silently ask Jesus to let his love flow in with each breath. As you exhale, picture that love flowing out with your breath, blessing the situation. Continue this all the time you're talking or listening or doing.

When school began one year, I told Fran she could drive one of the cars each day because she had to be at school by seven o'clock and was out at noon. If she were to ride the bus, she'd have to get up very early to catch it, and then she'd have quite a lot of time at school before classes began. I told her that it was a privilege to be able to take the car, and that I didn't want her to act as a taxi service for her friends after school because it would involve a good bit of time on her part and expense on mine. It never dawned on me that she might run a taxi service *en route* to school. I simply assumed that she'd sleep in until the last minute, then get up and go to school. I've found it's best not to make assumptions.

I learned one evening that she did taxi a friend now and then to school, a friend who lived out of the way, and the next morning she was planning to pick her up and take her to school.

As I was working in the kitchen I casually mentioned to her that she wasn't to take her friends to school, as well as not take them home after school. She looked stricken. She's prone to dramatics. "But I promised Kathy that I'd be by for her early tomorrow morning. We're going early to do a chemistry experiment."

"Well, you'll just have to call her and tell her she'll have to walk over here, that your old ogre of a mother won't let you drive and pick her up," I replied smiling.

"But she only lives a few blocks away," she wailed.

"Then it won't take her long to walk over," I said.

Immediately Fran began to throw all kinds of accusations at me. "You never let me—blah, blah, blah . . ." and "You always—blah, blah, blah . . ." She began to cry. I stood there relaxing my jaws, feeling a yawn in the back of my throat, picturing the love of Jesus pouring into and through me to Fran. I didn't feel upset at all, and I made no attempt to answer the accusations. I merely said, when there was a pause in the torrent of words, "Well, dear, you can talk till you're blue in the face if you want to, but you still can't pick Kathy up." She stormed downstairs to her room, sobbing dramatically. I finished my work in the kitchen and went up to my room. I could hear Fran wailing away below me. I was quite aware that she was aware that I could hear her. After about twenty minutes—and I wondered how she could sustain the emotional pitch so long—I went downstairs and said, my jaws relaxed and a yawn in the back of my throat, "Fran, you can have ten more minutes to cry, and if you can't be finished by then, you don't drive the car to school any morning." I spoke quietly, the love flowing through me, and I went back to my room.

In five minutes Fran was on the kitchen phone, tears all gone. Kathy wasn't at home, so she left the message with Kathy's sister and went back to her room. A little later Kathy called her to say it was okay because she couldn't have gone to school early anyway.

It just happened that I'd gone to the kitchen to get a drink of water when Kathy called Fran, and Fran told me what she'd said. I looked at her for a while and then said, "See, you got all upset and wasted all that emotion for nothing." She looked chagrined and came over to me, put her arms around me and laid her head on my shoulder and said, "I don't like it when I feel that way toward you."

"We usually get excited about things that aren't worth wasting our time on," I said, and we just held each other for a while, the reconciling, healing love of Jesus flowing through us.

Paul says to make love our aim. He doesn't say that everyone will respond to love. But the response isn't our business. Our business is to let love flow, regardless. Certainly Jesus loved, yet he was crucified. He who personified love is to be our way. He who is one with the Father is love, for God is love and we, when we love, are like him.

There are other situations in the day-by-dayness of life I could share with you, but I'm sure you get the idea. Tough love may be painful to you and to others. But if you hang in there you'll be stronger, and so will the others in the long run. When you've prayed about a situation and know what you feel is God's will about it, do it; but make love your aim as you do it.

Are you ready now to take a look into yourself and see what kind or kinds of games you've been playing under the guise of love? There may be a situation you're facing right now that could be eased if you'd relax and let the love, the tough love of Jesus flow through you.

Loving Father, I want the love that Paul talked about to the Corinthians, the kind of love that was manifested in Jesus, the kind of love that's you. I open myself now for you to cleanse me of all attitudes, emotions, actions, and reactions I've termed "love" but which aren't love at all. Then fill me to overflowing with your love. I choose now and in the future to make love my aim. Amen.

TEST THE SPIRITS

When you stop playing pious games and begin to grow where you're planted, when you get to know Jesus and learn to overcome disappointment, you begin to move into the abundant life that's available to a Christian. Yet you also may find that many times you're thwarted in living the life of love; other times you're given great help in living. So I think it's time to spend a little while on a subject which I consider important. It may be that what I'm going to share with you will test your credulity, but I can only report what's happened to me as I see it, how I've handled certain situations, and what conclusions I've reached. If it's helpful to you, fine; if not, simply file it away for a while as you may need it later.

I'm going to start by talking with you about Satan and evil spirits.

For the most part, the orthodox churches have pussyfooted around the subject or ignored it, while for the most part the Pentecostal churches have blown it up so much that they tremble and are filled with fear, seeing a devil behind every bush and in everyone whose behavior doesn't conform to theirs or whose doctrine differs with their own. It seems to me that there's a balanced, middle-of-the-road approach to the subject. Whether I've achieved a balance is debatable. Anyway, let's see what I have to say.

I first heard about evil spirits when I was twenty-one years old. At a conference I was attending, a man sitting at the dinner table began to relate some encounters he'd had with evil spirits. I shivered as he told his stories and hoped I'd never meet any evil spirits.

One night several months later I was alone. My roommate was out and I prepared for bed in my room at the dorm. I left the little light on over the picture of Jesus, walked by and closed my closet door, slipped into bed, and pulled the covers up. Suddenly my closet door burst open, and my clothes began to whip out as though a gale were blowing them, and a being appeared at the right side of my bed. I can only describe it as a "he" who was leering down at me. I was absolutely petrified and tried to cry out, but it was as though my vocal cords were paralyzed. I was so frightened that I fainted, and when I came to it was morning. I glanced at my closet and saw that it was open and that my clothes were tangled, so I knew it hadn't been a dream.

I talked with a very wise woman about what had happened, and she said, "You get down on your knees and pray that if anything like that should ever happen again that your mind will go immediately to Jesus, and you'll know you belong to him." Well, I got down on my knees right then and there and prayed as she suggested.

Nothing happened in the way of another encounter until several months later when I was staying a few weeks with a friend. She had said, "When you graduate, come and stay with me for a couple of weeks, and I'll serve you breakfast in bed every morning." I couldn't turn down an offer like that because I'd had an extremely full schedule that year and was in need of rest. Nettie had been in the guest room to have prayer with me and to wish me a goodnight. She'd turned out the light on her way out and I settled down under the covers. Then "he" was by my bed, leering at me. My mind went immediately to Jesus, and I knew I belonged to him. I began to chuckle, and I said in my mind, "You can't hurt me; I belong to Jesus," and "he" disappeared. I felt enveloped by the love of Jesus, and I dropped off to sleep.

During the next few months I talked with a number of people about Satan and evil spirits. It was our shared belief that they fled at the name of Jesus. One woman said that she just repeated "Jesus" over and over again when she was fearful, and she always became peaceful. We decided that we were safe if we looked only to Jesus.

When Kay was a baby, I got up every night in the middle of the night to go downstairs and heat a bottle of milk for her. One night as I came down, I'd just turned on the landing and was facing the archway to the living room when I was startled to see a woman standing in the archway. She was tall and slender, dressed in a long gray gown, her golden hair braided in a coronet on the top of her head. I immediately began to say the name "Jesus" quietly, and on each step I repeated it, yet she didn't go away. At the foot of the stairs I turned left toward the kitchen, switched on the light, got the bottle out of the refrigerator and heated it, saying "Jesus, Jesus, Jesus," all the time. I continued to say his name as I turned off the stove, took the bottle, wiped it dry, switched off the light, and started for the stairs. She was still there in the archway. All the way up the stairs,

I repeated Jesus' name. Every night for the next week the very same thing occurred, and then one night as I was on the next to the last step, it was as though her thought came into my mind, "I would never harm you," and I was engulfed in a wave of love. All fear left me. I went on out to the kitchen, and when I came back through to the stairway, she was gone. She never appeared again, but I've had contact with her in what I think is a most unusual way.

When we served a country pastorate in northern Illinois, it was my custom to spend an hour in the morning before the girls got up, an hour after lunch when they played outdoors, and an hour before going to sleep reading the Bible and some devotional book, meditating and praying. One day after lunch I went into the bedroom, shut and locked the door as was my custom, and as I walked toward the bed I was suddenly overwhelmed with a great yearning to do God's will, whatever it was. I went over to the bed, knelt beside it and laid my head and shoulders on it. I yearned to be used by God in anyway he wanted to use me. Then I heard myself speaking, only it wasn't I. The voice was much richer and deeper than mine. It was beautiful. It seemed to have a very slight accent. I listened in astonishment as the voice praised and thanked God and assured me that God had wonderful things planned for us. There was a knock at the door. One of the girls had come in from playing. I felt a contraction in my throat and when the voice came out, it was pitched higher to sound like me, and it said, "Just a moment, please," and I heard the little feet patter away. My throat relaxed. It came into my mind that perhaps the voice was that of the woman I'd seen in the archway several years before, but before I could formulate the question in my mind, the voice was answering me, "Yes, I am the woman. My name is Contina, and I help you as I can." Then she began again to praise and thank God, and my spirit soared within me in gratitude and thanksgiving. The voice assured me that God was taking care of us and was guiding us, that we were to trust him and that he would show us what to do. The voice then was silent, and I began to thank God for the beautiful experience, and I rededicated myself to him to go anywhere at anytime for him.

Not long after that we were led to leave the pastorate and move to New York city where Ted became a youth editor for Friendship Press, a part of the National Council of Churches.

As I see it, the difference in the encounters with the two spirits is that the first one was evil, causing me to be fearful. He later fled at the name of Jesus, whereas the second spirit was good, staying when the name of Jesus was used and then drawing me closer to God and deepening my commitment to him out of love.

Yes, there are evil spirits, and yes, there are good spirits. So it is wise to test the spirits as we're told to do by John. Read I John 4:1-4. He tells you how to test the spirits.

As your own spiritual life deepens, you'll be open to both good and evil spirits, but you need have no fear. You can claim the protection of Jesus. I recommend that you do this on awakening, before meditation and prayer time, and before sleeping. You can be wrapped around and filled by his presence and be as a fortress, impregnable.

I believe we're surrounded by a great cloud of witnesses and that if we ignore these witnesses, we're missing out on a real enrichment for our lives. Now don't get me wrong, I'm not suggesting that you try to make contact with a specific person you love who's dead, yet if someone comes to you, don't be afraid. Timothy tells us that we're not given a spirit of cowardice or fear but a spirit of power and love and calm and a well-balanced mind.

When Mother Kimmel died, the girls and I went to Pennsylvania for her funeral. I was in my brother-in-law's garage, spray-painting a pair of Fran's yellow shoes, getting them ready for her to wear to the funeral, when I felt someone had come into the garage. Thinking it might be one of my daughters, I turned around. I saw Ted, his mother, and his father. The three of them were standing with their arms around each other, Ted on the right, Mother in the middle, and Dad on the left. They were smiling at me, and the very air around them seemed moving in joyousness as though their happiness at being together was something they couldn't contain. Mother and Dad looked about thirty years old, much as they looked in pictures I'd seen of them taken when their sons were small. A sense of joy and peace filled me, and I smiled. Then they weren't there. I turned back to the shoes and finished spraying them. I was caught up in happiness and thankfulness to God.

If you're still with me and your credulity isn't stretched too far, let me share another happening with you.

While I was visiting friends in Puerto Rico, they were asked to pray for a man who had many problems. The three of us took the man and his wife up to a mountain cabin occupied by a Pentecostal woman to ask her to pray, too. Since I didn't speak Spanish, I drew over into a corner to be in prayer as the four of them prayed for the man. Then a really strange thing happened as I looked at him. I saw another man inside him, and my thoughts began to go out to the spirit in him. They were such thoughts as "This man can never satisfy you, only Jesus can. Why don't you come to Jesus? He wants to give you the desires of your heart. He's yearning to give you all you need and want. He's standing here beside you. Come to him and be satisfied." I seemed an observer, divorced from the thoughts which flowed through my mind to the possessing spirit. As I watched the wooing of the spirit, he began to rise very slowly out of the man until he was completely out. I saw Jesus there beside him, and I watched the two of them walk to the doorway together, go through it, descend the step, and walk down the path until they were out of sight. I looked back at the man and saw other spirits in him but the group around him finished praying, and we left.

I do believe that some people are possessed. I also believe that there are evil, unlightened, mischievous spirits that can be attached to people without possessing them. For instance, I once saw what appeared to be a big lump of darkness on the back of a man. The man was going into a prayer room. This big lump jumped off the man's back and moved down the hallway. It was attached to the man by what looked like a cord. I seemed to catch its thought, "You go on and have your little prayer time. I'll be here when you come back out." At the time I had no idea how to deal with anything like this, and I didn't seem to have sense enough to say, "Jesus, what do I do now?"

I believe that there are spirits of gluttony, jealousy, pride, and other things that can either attach themselves to people or can really possess them. We have authority to command them, in the name of Jesus, to leave. However, I must put in a warning here. We need to be led by the Lord in working with and counseling people. We need to seek wisdom and above all, love. If someone you know is acting in an abnormal way, don't jump to the conclusion that he's possessed. Perhaps all he needs is to get more sleep or perhaps something is physically wrong with him that a good doctor could correct. I remember reading about a prayer group which met weekly for prayer, and when the meeting was over, a number of people remained for another session of prayer, speaking in tongues and casting out demons. One evening the group spent hours working with a young woman, trying to cast out a demon, but they didn't have any success. She died the following day. An autopsy revealed a tumor on the brain which had been causing her to act abnormally. If she'd gone to a doctor, she might have been healed. If the people praying for her, trying to cast out the demon, had prayed for wisdom, they might have acted differently. So let the casting out of demons, the freeing of people, be one of the many acts of God through you, if he wants this. But don't make it your whole life. Be balanced.

A doctor friend said that balance is needed in everything. When he hits his finger with a hammer, instead of saying, "Darn it," he says "Balance!" He feels that most of our problems stem from the fact that we get out of balance physically, emotionally, mentally, or spiritually. I agree with him. I even think you can spend too much time reading the Bible, going to church meetings, praying, trying to find God's will for your life. You can get spiritual indigestion. I've seen it happen, and it's taken months of counseling to get into balance and harmony again. You're here to live in the world and to live abundantly on all planes—physical, mental, emotional, and spiritual. See that you have a balanced life. The truly spiritual person is one who delights in the whole of life, not just those things we've piously dubbed "spiritual."

Now there's something I want to share with you. I've found it to be extremely practical. The Church of England has an exorcism service. I sat in on such a service one day and decided to adapt it for use for myself, in my counseling and in my prayer groups and prayer labs.

Most of us stay close enough to Jesus most of

the time that we don't need to fear we'll be possessed, but I find, even in the most holy of us, that we can become proud, self-righteous, critical, angry, resentful, fearful, and self-satisfied. So I've adapted the exorcism service to be used to cleanse people from negativism of any sort, and it works.

Take a glass of water and hold it, asking God to bless it. Imagine his blessing streaming into it. Then dip your finger into the water and draw a small cross with a circle around it on the forehead of the person you're cleansing and say, "I cleanse you (and say the person's name) in the name of Jesus." Dip in the water again and make the sign of the cross with a circle around it on the nape of the neck and say the same words again. Dip in the water a third time and make the sign of the cross with the circle around it on the person's solar plexus, over the clothes he's wearing, and say the words again. Then again dip a finger into the water and make the sign of the cross and the circle around it at the base of the spine and repeat the words. Then set the glass down and lay your hands on the person's head and thank God for cleansing him, and ask him to fill him with his love and wholeness.

You cleanse a house in a similar way, making the sign of the cross with a circle around it on each wall of each room and on a corner of each mirror hanging on a wall or attached to a chest. Each time you draw the symbol, say, "I cleanse this room in the name of Jesus." After going through the house, give a prayer of thanks that God has cleansed the house, and ask him to fill it with his love and wholeness. You'll notice a difference immediately in the atmosphere of your home. I've found that in my own home there comes more harmony among family members and more creativity in relationships.

How farfetched this must sound to some of you. But let me assure you that the unseen world of the spirit is very real. If you're filled with God's love you won't have any fear of the spirits, evil or good. Perfect love casts out fear.

Don't deliberately set out to look for Satan and evil spirits. Somehow we usually find what we're looking for, and certainly don't say, off the top of your head, "That's of the devil," or "That's Antichrist." Pray for wisdom and for the gift of discernment if you are to be given it. There's enough evil in the world which will make itself known to you without your having to go turn up stones to see if it's under them; so relax, become aware of the angels and archangels and the company of heaven that also surround you, and let your heart and mind be filled with praise and thanksgiving.

Loving Father, thank you for your power available to us through the name of Jesus. Thank you for being in us and for being greater than anything that's outside of us. Thank you for the balance we're moving into, and thank you for showing us ways in which we can wholeheartedly cooperate with your loving, cleansing, redeeming Spirit. Amen.

BE WHOLE

In counseling with people who are ill, one of the first questions I've learned to ask is the one Jesus also asked, "Do you want to be whole?" You'd think that anyone who's sick would want to be well, wouldn't you? Yet I've discovered that there are people who don't really know if they want to be well, and there are some who want to be sick. Sickness can be a game, a very costly game.

Ever since I started reading about psychosomatic illnesses in the fifties, I've seen statistics on the percentage of people who have nothing organically wrong with them, but who are sick. The percentage has stayed around the same over the years.

Several doctors I've talked with also confirm the percentage. Around 80 to 85 percent of the people who are ill have nothing organically wrong; their illnesses stem from unhappinness in the psyche or soul and eventually are manifest in the body.

Now please don't jump to the conclusion that there are no sick people. There are, and it's extremely difficult to pinpoint why some people are sick when the doctor can find no cause for their sickness. Those who are ill because of a sick soul manifest physical symptoms which are painful. Too often those of us who have a little knowledge about psychosomatic ills think that everyone is sick because of unhealthy emotions, and we make sweeping statements such as, "It's all in her mind." Just as we can't say that all abnormal behavior is demon possession, neither can we say that all illnesses stem from emotional problems.

There are places where teams of doctors, psychologists, and ministers seek to minister to the whole person—body, mind, and spirit. I think we're coming to see that a person needs balance in all three areas. I believe that we need to use every tool available to us in seeking wholeness. Since I'm no doctor or psychologist, I look at a person through the eyes of my own experience. I know that many of my ills have sprung from my emotions. When I begin to feel sick, I immediately check my emotions and my desires. I've averted several colds by doing so, because I've realized that a cold would be a good excuse for going to bed for a day or two, and I wouldn't have to cook meals or accept responsibilities for a while. When I've made up my mind to sleep late a few mornings and to eat our meals out and to forget about having to clean the house or do the laundry, miraculously the cold has cleared up. So, for myself, I know that colds can be averted.

Not long ago my daughter Fran was tempted to stay home from school and be sick. She'd had a full weekend of activities and had begun the week of school tired. She developed a bit of a sore throat; then she confessed to me that she'd like to be sick so she could stay home and rest, but that she hated to get behind in chemistry. As we talked, I shared with her that I'd like to have stayed in bed all day the day before but that there had been so many interesting things going on that I didn't want to miss that I'd rejected the bed idea, had done the interesting things during the day and early evening but had gotten home early and gone to bed to get a good night's sleep. She decided to do the same thing, and do you know, the sore throat cleared up.

I really believe that one reason we get sick is because we're not involved enough in living life and serving others. We have too much time to be introspective, and we use the introspection negatively, feeling sorry for ourselves or feeling resentful that certain things have happened to us which we don't think we deserve.

Mother Kimmel had arthritis and a heart condition. She and I talked very deeply one day. I shared with her some of my ideas about how illnesses can be very real, yet spring from negative emotions in us. She'd read widely and knew what I was talking about. I told her of the time when I'd had arthritic pain that was excruciating in a finger and that I'd tried to check into my emotions to see if I held any resentment toward anyone. About that time Susan had poison ivy which covered one eye and the side of her face and had spread down her body. As I bathed her eye open one morning I knew that I resented her, not only for requiring so much of my time then, but all the time. Suddenly I realized that I was all she had in the world, the only person to serve her, and a great wave of love swept into me and seemed to lift out the resentment, and I felt an overwhelming tenderness for her and for her dependency on me. A new gentleness came into my hands as I ministered to her and into my voice as I spoke to her. My finger never hurt after that experience.

Mother Kimmel then told me that she resented

God for taking her husband and for taking Ted, my husband and her youngest son, in a plane crash. And she said, "I just can't help being resentful." I tried to talk with her about how she could release her resentment, but she said again that she just couldn't help being resentful. I tried to share with her my idea of God, a loving father who, rather than punishing his children, delighted in giving them good gifts, but she still felt that he'd taken two precious people from her. I had to leave her and return to my home in another state. She died soon after our visit.

A very sick woman who asked to talk with me revealed that she had committed a very grave error thirty years before and hadn't been able to forgive herself for it. Her guilt ate away at her. I tried to share some scripture with her about forgiveness, and even though she said she believed that God had forgiven her, she said she just couldn't forgive herself.

Another woman vacillated between wanting to live and wanting to die. One day I said to her, "Do you really want to live? Do you really want to be whole?" and she answered, "I just don't know. Sometimes I think my family would be better off without me." She must have finally cast her vote for dying.

You've probably known some people who've

set a kind of deadline—and that's an interesting word, isn't it—for themselves. "If I can just hold out until the children get through school, . . ." and they do hold out until the children get through school, and then they die. Can we lay down our lives? Can we choose, deliberately, to die? There are a lot of unanswered questions concerning life and death, aren't there? It's not simple, is it? Not black or white, but infinite shades of gray. What complex beings we are. There are no snap judgments we can make, no hard and fast rules about illness and the cause of it.

A woman who was desperately ill asked me to pray that she'd be released to death. I prayed for God's will to be done, and she was healed.

A man asked me to visit him in the hospital one day. We talked a while, and I was led to take him through the prayer for the healing of the memories. I believe he was healed emotionally. Several days later he was released from the hospital.

A woman became very ill. Her husband was working in another state, and she and their children were living with his mother until he could find a suitable house or apartment. She became very short of breath, had to sleep propped up in bed, and she coughed a great deal. She went to the doctor who couldn't find anything really wrong

with her, but he began to give her injections daily
to build up her strength.

Her mother-in-law took care of the children and
pampered her by serving her excellent meals in
bed. The days went by and she got no better. In
fact, she found that she was enjoying the attention she was getting. Although it was uncomfort-
able to be short of breath and to cough so much,
the spells didn't last long, and she did like being
fussed over, and it was good not to have the full
responsibility of the children. They only came in
for a few minutes a day, so as not to tire her.
Actually, she was getting the first real rest she'd
had in years. Some days when she went in to see
the doctor, she made stops at the local library and
took books home to read while propped up in bed.
When she'd exhausted the little library's supply of
books, she remembered a book she'd had for years
but had never read. It was packed away in the
basement. While reading the book which dealt
with sickness and healing, it dawned on her that
she'd become filled with self-pity. After all, her
husband was in a large city, footloose and fancy-
free, and there she was cooped up on a farm with
three small children. It just wasn't fair that all
that responsibility should fall on her. Her eyes
filled with tears, and she glanced out the window.

The sunlight was blazing, and there was a glory on every tree that was just starting to leaf. The pond shimmered in the brightness of the light and suddenly she wanted to be well, to get out of doors and enjoy the beautiful springtime and to play with her children, hold them close and care for them. She'd cast her vote for life and wholeness, and she was healed in that shining instant. She got up, dressed, and went downstairs. I happen to be that woman.

I can't make any claims about knowing much about the workings of the mind, either the conscious or subconscious mind, but I have read quite a bit on the subject because it's so fascinating. I don't dig into very technical books, but into the popular books that are available.

In *Psycho-cybernetics* by Maxwell Maltz there are some very interesting examples of the power of the mind, both conscious and subconscious. In *Let's Believe,* a book for children but one from which many of us adults have gained a great deal, Agnes Sanford talks of the subconscious mind as "Junior," and she tells how to encourage him to help you. Karlins and Andrews in *Biofeedback* report, among other things, how blood pressure can be lowered by thinking.

Paul tells us to be transformed by the renewing

of our minds and to think of things which are pure and true, just and honorable, lovely and praiseworthy. I think he got hold of the idea that the mind is to be controlled or harnessed to bring blessings to us. James, you know, suggests that the tongue be brought under control so that it might bless rather than curse. Wouldn't it be wise of us to look into our own thoughts and our own words to see if they're helping us or hindering us?

I know people who play a seemingly endless tape of grievances and anxieties in their conversations. And from what I've discovered by talking with them, the tape goes on in their minds most of the time. Some of them are learning to control their minds and tongues by replacing destructive thoughts and words with constructive ones. One of my pet phrases used to be "I'm just fed up . . ." until I realized one day that I was never hungry. I always felt full. I learned not to use the phrase. A friend used to say, "It just tears me apart . . ." and then wondered why he developed a hole in his esophagus until I pointed out to him that his "Junior" was working hard for him, after having heard him say the phrase so much.

What about you? What are your pet phrases? What is your problem right now? Can you make any correlation between what you say and think and how you are physically? Don't be ashamed to

admit to certain thoughts and feelings just because
you think a Christian shouldn't have them.

Just as an alcoholic is ready for help when he
finally admits he's drinking too much, so you,
when you finally admit to having negative emotions, attitudes, thoughts, and words, can be helped.
The reforming alcoholic learns to resist the temptation to drink. He knows that when he does
weaken, there's always someone to call on to help
him. He learns to refuse to take a drink. Well, you
can resist the temptation to destructive emotions,
attitudes, thoughts, and words by refusing to have
anything to do with them, and you can replace
them with positive, constructive emotions, attitudes, thoughts, and words.

Do I hear some of you saying, "Just where does
this put Jesus if you do it all yourself? It leaves
him out, doesn't it?" Not at all. As you begin to
work out your own salvation, he's there to aid
you. You can turn to him in your thoughts. He's
been with you always, but you've ignored him.
You've thought for yourself and said what you've
pleased, and you've let negative emotions play
through your body or build up in your body. He
was left out then, wasn't he? But now you can
turn to him in faith that he can and will help you
to be whole.

The house that's all wired for electricity remains dark until someone presses the light switch. As long as you wait for the light to come on automatically without any help from you, the light stays off. Well, Jesus is available with tremendous power, but you have to initiate the contact. You have to press the switch to show him that you're open and receptive to his help. The switch is prayer coupled with faith. You've learned that on your own you can't make it, but that you can make it with his strength and power. Couple that faith with prayer and you can be made whole and can stay whole.

By all means, if you are ill, see a competent doctor. God uses doctors in wonderful ways to restore health and wholeness in people. I certainly see a doctor when I'm ill. Doctors work with God. Learn to cooperate with God in as many ways as possible to be whole. A healthy attitude or a merry heart, as the writer of Proverbs says, does good like a medicine. So cultivate, with the help of Jesus, a merry heart, one free from self-pity and self-condemnation and resentment and bitterness.

Loving Father, thank you for your healing power available to me. I need it for I want to be made whole. I want to stop playing "The Sickness" game. Take over my thoughts and attitudes, my emotions and words. Cleanse them and redeem them, and help me to begin thinking your thoughts and saying your words and experiencing the fruit of the spirit—the harmony of love, the power of peace, the gaiety of joy, and above all the real freedom through self-control. Amen.

ASK AND IT'LL
BE GIVEN YOU

There's a story I want to share with you. I heard it a number of years ago, but as I go over it time after time I seem to see more and more in it. It's about a man named Pete who had been imprisoned unjustly. He was considered dangerous by the authorities, so he was closely guarded. One report I heard said that sixteen guards were used, and another report said eighty, so I'm really not sure, and it probably doesn't matter anyway. Let's just say that he was heavily guarded and let it go at that. Oh, yes, at night they always took extra precautions by double-chaining him between two guards.

Pete had been a member of a prayer group for

quite some time, and when the group heard he'd been imprisoned, it set up all-night prayer vigils for him in the home of one of the women. The group was sure he'd done nothing wrong.

Well, one night Pete was awakened by someone shaking his shoulder. It was hard for him to get his eyes open because the room was flooded with bright light. He didn't know what was going on, whether he'd be taken for grilling or what. He was told to get up, and as he did, he felt the chains fall off. He thought that the guards had unlocked the chains, and he stood, trying to get his eyes open and rubbing his wrists. It was sore where the chains had rubbed. He was told to get dressed and to put his shoes on. Still in a daze, he slipped into his clothes with his eyes half open and put on his shoes. He later reported that this all seemed like a dream or a vision to him. It didn't seem real. He followed the person who'd awakened him, and they walked out of the cell, past several cell blocks and out of the prison, across the yard to the big iron gate in the wall. The gate swung open as they approached it, and they walked through it and on down the street several blocks when suddenly Pete realized that he was alone. He looked around but couldn't see anyone anywhere; the street was completely deserted. It dawned on him that he was really out of prison, that he was free. An angel must have helped him escape.

Well, you can imagine how happy he was—he was a free man—but if he wanted to stay that way, he'd better get a move on. So he hurried over to his friend Mary's house where he knew he'd find help to get out of the city before it was discovered that he'd escaped. He quickly walked to Mary's and rapped on the door. Finally he roused the maid who came and called out, "Who is it?" When Pete told her, she let out a squeal of delight. Instead of unlocking the door and letting him in, she ran into the room where the prayer group was meeting and sang out, "Mr. Pete's at the door, Mr. Pete's at the door!" The people gathered for prayer were stunned at her outburst, thinking she'd taken leave of her senses, and one of them said to her, "You must be out of your mind!" But she kept saying that he was really there. Finally one of them, no doubt to humor her, said, "Maybe it's his ghost," but she urged them to come and see. They then heard a pounding on the front door and rushed out to it. Someone unlocked the door and opened it, and there was Pete. Believe me, they were absolutely amazed to see him, and they pulled him inside, shut the door, and began to question him, one person's question tumbling over another's. He quieted them and told them the story

I've told you. He told them to tell Jim and the others who weren't there. He said he'd go into hiding for a few days and then leave the city, and he left them.

The story I've shared with you is recorded in Acts 12:6-17. The Acts and the Gospels are filled with exciting stories about answered prayer, answered often in ways to astonish the people praying. Jesus continually revealed God as a loving father who desires to give good gifts to his children. He said to ask, and it would be given; he said to pray, believing you're receiving.

Many of us grew up under the admonition not to be selfish in our prayers by praying for things that we want, and we grew up under the question, "What do you think God is, a celestial bellboy?" We play the game of "I'm Unworthy." But Jesus said if a child asked his father for a loaf of bread would he be given a stone instead, or if he asked for a fish would he be given a poisonous snake. Then he went on to say that our father in heaven even more surely will give good gifts to those who ask him for them. Then he revealed the loving heart of God in a story about a forgiving father.

A young man went to his father one day and said, "Dad, I've been thinking. I believe I'd like to have my share of the estate now rather than after you're gone. I want to be out on my own; I want to see the world and live a little."

Now the father could have said, "Son, I don't know what the future holds for me financially, and although I'd like to be able to divide the estate now, I need every penny I have in order to keep the place running now and to prepare for my old age so I won't be dependent on anyone." Or he could have said, "I know what you'll do with the money since you don't have any business sense at all. You'll squander it, and then what will you do—come back to me and want more? Well, once you're on your own, whatever bed you make, you'll have to lie in it," or even, "No, son, you're irresponsible with money. I've spent my lifetime building this estate. For your own good I've set up everything in a trust, and if I should die tomorrow, you're well provided for under the trust. Of course, you won't actually handle the money until you're thirty." But he didn't say any of these very reasonable answers. Instead, he looked with eyes of understanding on his son, loving him dearly and wanting with all his being to shield and protect the young man. Nevertheless, he divided his estate and gave his son his share and wished him well.

After the son left I think the father must have hired several servants just to stand watch on the road in the event that his son returned, because later, when the young man realized how much better off even the servants in his father's house were than he was and started for home, word came to the father while the son was quite a distance away that he was returning.

Now the father could have gone on about his work muttering, "Guess the young scoundrel ran through his money and now wants more. Well, he won't get it, I'll tell you, no sir, he won't get it, not if he comes begging me." Or he could have said with an all-knowing look, "Just as I predicted! I told everybody it was a fool-crazy idea for that kid to go off like that. I knew he'd come to no good end, and I was right. Now maybe he'll buckle down and get to work." Or he might have said, "Probably do him good if I don't pay any attention to him. After all, he made his bed, let him lie in it." But he didn't. His father's heart welled up with love, and he literally ran down the road, a most undignified act for a man of his age and position in life, his robes flying in the wind, several servants trailing him. When he got near enough to his son, he shouted joyously, "Son, you've come home!" He ran on to him and hugged him and kissed him. Even while the son was trying to give the little speech he'd prepared and rehearsed until he knew it by heart to let his father know why he'd come home, the delighted father didn't pay any attention to his words but looked at him, saw his ragged condition, and commanded the servants to get the finest robe in the house and bring it for his son. As the servants ran ahead to get the robe, the father called out, "Mind you, get the finest and bring sandals, too—also my signet ring. I want to place it on his finger, so he can wear it once again and have all my wealth at his disposal. And listen, have some of the men kill the calf we've been fattening for this very occasion." Turning to his son, he said, "We're going to throw the biggest party you ever saw." With his arm around the shoulders of his bewildered son, the two of them headed for the house. "And, son, after you've bathed and rested, you let the servants dress you and then come on into the courtyard; by then word will have been sent to the neighbors that you've come home, and they'll be here to see you and welcome you and enjoy the feast and music. Oh, son, it's as though you'd been dead and had come back to life. It's so good to see you. I'm so glad you've come home!"

Do you see the glad, loving heart of the father, wanting to give far above anything the son could have asked or wished for? Do you see that this is the way God, our loving father gives, full measure, pressed down, heaped up and running over, and then continues to pour and pour and pour, far beyond anything we could ask or dream? And we think it's selfish to ask him for good things? We think that our asking would turn God into a celestial bellboy? How far we've missed the loving heart of the father who would pour out his good gifts on us, if we'd only ask.

"Fine," you say, "but I've asked God for certain things, and I didn't get what I wanted. How do you account for that?"

We must realize that God answers prayer in a number of ways. He says yes, and he says no, and he says wait. The "yes" comes when our prayer is in total agreement with his will, and without anything having to be worked out, our prayer is answered immediately. Not long ago a woman came to a prayer group I'm in. She had a great deal of pain in her arm and side. We laid our hands on her and prayed for the pain to be removed. That prayer was answered yes, and was answered immediately.

When we thought about moving from Indiana to warmer climate, I made a prayer tree. I put thirteen items that I wanted on that prayer tree. Six months later eleven had been answered yes. The other two have been answered no, and I see the wisdom of this now. When he answered no, he had something better for me than I dreamed of.

I was talking with a group of women one day

about prayer, and one woman told us that for several years she pleaded with God to save her marriage. Sometimes her pleading was so intense that she'd be driving in traffic and suddenly just stop the car to plead with God to save her marriage. She said she finally realized that God had said no, and she allowed the divorce to go through. God wiped the bitterness out of her and helped her make a life for herself.

When I was in Lourdes at the healing shrine, I met a group of people from a Catholic church in England. One of the women told me why approximately thirty people from their parish go to Lourdes each year to help push people on carts or in wheelchairs or just help as they can anyone who's crippled or in need of help. A man in their congregation had made a pilgrimage each year to Lourdes for seventeen years, hoping to be healed. On the seventeenth year, he was healed. A group from his church go each year at vacation time in praise and thanksgiving to God for healing their friend.

Now I don't know why the healing didn't happen the very first year, or why seventeen years went by before the healing occurred. I just know that sometimes God says wait.

When I was about eleven years old, I wanted a bicycle very much. I prayed every night for a bicycle for Christmas, and of course, I let my parents know what I wanted. I just knew I'd get a bike for Christmas, but I didn't. I received a football and several other gifts. I was just sick with disappointment. But I brightened, because I had a birthday in February and that's when I'd get the bike, but when my birthday rolled around, no bike came. But one beautiful spring day, when the snow had melted and the ground had dried out and the air was warm, I got my bicycle, a beautiful brown and gold one, more shining and glorious than the red one I had longed for so earnestly. My parents had withheld a bike because circumstances weren't right to have it and use it when I'd wanted it at Christmas and my birthday. At just the right time, they gave me the bike. Perhaps we're premature in what we want, and circumstances have to be worked out just right in order for the answer to come. Rather than seeking any gift, I'm learning to seek only the giver, allowing his wisdom to give me what is best. I do let God know what I'd like, but I'm always willing to take his good gifts that I wouldn't even have thought of. I'm like the son, overwhelmed by the goodness of the father who gives so freely and lovingly.

Just as I want my daughters to share with me what they dream and desire so that I can help them and bless them, so God wants you and me to come to him and share with him our dreams and desires. Nothing is too small nor too large to bring to the loving Father. If we come to him in the spirit of Jesus—as willing as Jesus was when he prayed that the cup might pass from him yet not his will, but the Father's be done—we can be assured that when the answer is no or wait that God has something better in store for us. The death of Jesus wasn't defeat for him; it was necessary in order that he might carry out the plan of God for the benefit of mankind.

There are times when we just don't know how to pray. When this happens, the best way to pray is to release the person or situation into the hands of God for him to work his perfect will out, whatever it may be.

After my quiet time one day I decided that I'd drop by the office and pick up any mail that might have come for me. I planned to stop by a cleaning shop on the way and leave Kay's and Susan's velvet dresses to be pressed. I headed down the freeway and got off at Northern Avenue, turned in at the cleaners, and went in with the dresses. The woman behind the counter was busy with a customer, and I waited. After the customer left, the woman turned to me, and I said, "These dresses just need to be pressed; they're not dirty. They've been packed away for a while."

The woman looked at me oddly and said, "Well, I don't know whether or not I should accept them." I must say that I felt somewhat strange because I'd been in there before and left things, and I couldn't imagine why she might not take the dresses. "Ahh, what do you mean?" I asked. "Well," she hesitated, "I don't know how much longer I'll be in business." She swallowed hard. "I may go into bankruptcy." Tears came into her eyes. I looked at her and said, "What's your name?" "Julia," she replied. "Julia, do you ever pray?" I asked. "Oh, yes," she said, "I believe in prayer." "Well," I questioned her, "do you believe that God's will is good?" "Oh, yes," she said. "Then why don't we just thank and praise God that his perfect will is going to be done in your business? If he wants you to keep it open, then he can work everything out for you to stay open, and if he has something better for you, he'll let you go bankrupt. Do you agree?" She looked into my eyes a long time and then smiled and said, "Yes." I peeled off my gloves and we took hands across the counter, and I prayed that God's will be done, whatever it was. If he wanted her to make a go of the cleaning shop and help the community by providing a service, then he'd have to see to it that the shop stayed open; and if he had a better plan for her, doing some other work somewhere else, that he'd let her go bankrupt. I thanked and praised him that his will would be done. When I finished the prayer, Julia gripped my hands tightly and said, "Do you know that God sent you to me today?" I answered, "I believe he did." Then I fished out one of my cards from my purse and said, "If you ever want to pray or talk, call me. Bless you," and I picked up the two little dresses and went out of the shop. The outcome of the story is that the business was still going months later. I saw recently that the road was being torn up to widen the street there, so I don't know what's happening. If Julia wants to talk or pray, she can call.

A woman whose daughter-in-law had been healed through prayer called me one day, and we talked about her son in Germany. He and his wife were expecting a baby, and it was due soon. The grandmother-to-be was very happy and excited, expecting to get a call at any time from her son, telling her about the birth of her grandchild.

Several days after talking with the woman, I left on a trip. I was to do several prayer labs in various cities and end up in North Manchester, Indiana, with a friend for a few days. As I was walking into the friend's home, my suitcase in hand, the phone was ringing. Wini answered it and said it was for me. The grandmother-to-be was on the line. The baby had arrived, a beautiful boy, but he wasn't expected to live. Her son had called to tell her, and he'd said, "Could you ask that woman who prayed for Carla to be healed to pray for Baby Robert?" So she rang up my daughters back in Phoenix, and they gave her my schedule, and she called to ask for prayer. My heart sank, for I knew I couldn't do anything for that precious little baby way across the ocean, but I knew God was a loving father and that he could be trusted, and I said, "We don't know what God's will is for Baby Robert, whether it's to take him or to leave him. Since we know beyond a shadow of a doubt that his will is always for the best, can we just release Baby Robert into his hands for his perfect will to be done?" She agreed, and I prayed, turning the baby over to God for him to have his way with, whatever it was. Then I said to her, "Let's just keep thanking God that his will is being done every time we think of Baby Robert." Then we said good-bye. I later found out that at the time we were praying, little Robert took a turn for the better and began to recover. He's a strong, healthy boy today.

Ask and it will be given you. Ask for what you want, and then tell God that if he has something better you'll take that instead. If you don't know what to ask for, simply turn the situation over to him and ask for his will to be done; then when you think about the situation, just thank him that his will is being done, even if it means thanking him several hundred times each day. "The reason you don't have what you want is that you don't ask God for it" (James 4:2). "Ask and you will be given what you ask for" (Matt. 7:7).

You don't have to play the "I'm Unworthy" game. No one's "worthy." God in his grace gives us far above anything we could dream of. He always gives full measure, pressed down, heaped up, and overflowing.

Loving Father, help me to look over my list of needs and desires and then bring them to you. Help me not to settle for less than your will, for I'm learning that your will is always for the best. Thanks, Father. Amen.

GIVE THANKS
IN ALL THINGS

Probably the one person doing more to spread thanksgiving and praise than anyone else at the present is a rather slight, joyful man by the name of Merlin Carothers. I think his book, *Power in Praise*, is especially good in showing us how to give thanks in all situations. I know many people who've been blessed by his ministry.

I must admit that my life has been on an even keel for several years. What little things have come up, I've been able to cope with, seeking God's wisdom and strength. There hasn't been anything so terrible that couldn't be worked out fairly easily, but one day I faced a situation unlike any I'd ever faced before.

It happened on one of the most beautiful Sundays that year in Arizona. My daughters and I had been to church school and worship and then had lunched with friends. It was a glorious day, sunny and warm with a slight breeze blowing, and as I swung the VW camper into our driveway, I saw the front of the house with the paint peeling on it. "Today is the day I get out there and scrape that paint off and put on the primer," I said.

I slipped into an old pair of blue slacks, donned my blue sweatshirt, and gathered together the things I needed for the job. I took a chair from the bridge set and a short-handled spatula from the kitchen—as you can see I wasn't daunted by not having a ladder or proper paint scraper. I propped the chair on what I thought was firm footing and climbed onto it. I began to scrape the peeling paint, humming with happiness. It didn't take very long to finish the job; I got down, went into the garage to see where the can of primer was, found it, opened it, stirred it, found a paint brush, and headed for the front of the house. However, I faced a problem. I wouldn't be able to hang on to the house, hold the paint can, and wield the paint brush. For that I'd need at least three hands, so I asked Kay if she'd come and hold the can for me. As I was dipping my brush into the paint can, about halfway through the job, my body twisted

around, tipping the chair off balance and the chair
started to go down. Instinctively I reached around
to grab something, and I pulled the metal back of
the chair into my left side at my ribs, and I went
thud onto the ground, the breath knocked out of
me. I lay there a bit, trying to breathe and not
wanting to frighten Kay. I tried to assure her
between gasps for air that I was really okay. When
I could breathe again, I got up and gingerly made
my way into the house and sat on the sofa in the
living room. I really didn't sit upright because of
the pain in my ribs; I sat at a forty-five degree
angle from the floor, my feet stretched out in front
of me. To try to take a long deep breath was agony,
a sharp pain stabbing me in the left side whenever I tried. By now Fran and Susan had heard the
commotion and were in the living room. Fran
slipped a cool hand under my sweatshirt and laid
it on my ribs, and it felt so good.

I tried to reassure the girls that I was all right,
just a bit breathless and hurting some, but that I
really felt well enough to go back outside and
finish the priming job. After all, there wasn't much
left to do, so back outside Kay and I went; I
finished the job, hurting ever so much, put the
primer away, cleaned the paint brush, and hung
it up.

I decided to fill the tub with hot water and soak

in it. I found out later that dry heat, not wet, was what I should have used. I must have soaked for at least half an hour, but somehow the pain hadn't eased the way I'd thought it would.

A man in our church who is a chiropractor is sometimes in his office on Sunday. I called him, but he said he wouldn't be able to see me for at least an hour, so I waited, trying to find a comfortable position in which to stand or sit or lie, and I never did. When it was time to start for the office, I had quite a painful time getting into the Pinto. The fifteen-mile ride to the doctor's office wasn't exactly painless.

John took me into an examining room and poked, pulled, and twisted me. He decided it wasn't necessary to take x-rays since the treatment would be the same for broken, cracked, or bruised ribs. He thought I had a deep bruise, so he put a wide elastic band around my midriff and pulled it very tight. The pain eased.

But when I got home, I realized the band was too tight. I couldn't sit or lie comfortably in it so I loosened it, prepared supper, then went upstairs to lie down while the children ate; but again there was no relief from the pain. I turned one way and then another. I tried a pillow under the small of my back. Nothing helped. There was no relief. Around ten o'clock I thought I'd better take a couple of aspirin. I don't know why I dislike taking any kind of medication, but I do, and I'll put off taking it as long as possible. Well, I got off the bed very slowly and was walking along the foot of it when it suddenly occurred to me that I'd just read *Power in Praise* the day before, and that I was to thank and praise God for the pain. I really wasn't at all grateful for the pain, but I began to thank him with my lips, walking back and forth at the foot of the bed, tears streaming down my face, holding my side, gasping in short breaths between words, "Thank—you—Father—thank—you —oh—thank—you." I continued for approximately ten minutes; then I realized that the pain had subsided. Very cautiously, while still thanking God, I moved around the end of the bed and carefully slid between the sheets. I thought about reaching up to turn out the light on my bedside table, but I rejected the idea immediately thinking, "Let sleeping pains lie!" I closed my eyes and continued to thank God in my mind. I must have fallen asleep, because the next thing I knew it was six in the morning. I'd slept the whole night through. The pain was never excruciating again. Oh, I was aware of an ache, and I couldn't turn too quickly for several weeks, and sometimes when I'd been sitting a long time a pain would start, but I'd just begin saying thank you again, and it would leave.

My firsthand experience with thanking God for whatever is bad or hurtful in my life showed me that it really worked. What Merlin Carothers had written had worked for me when I put his idea into practice.

Wherever I've gone to talk to groups or to lead prayer labs, I've shared the idea of thanking God for whatever hurts physically, emotionally, mentally, or spiritually. Maybe someday we'll know just what law is released to work when we begin to praise and thank God for a situation that formerly we'd have moaned and groaned over. Perhaps our getting our eyes off the problem and onto God gives him room to move into the situation to bring it into harmony with his will.

A woman in a group where I shared the story of my falling off the chair began to thank God for the arthritis she had in her hands. Later during our time together, she told us that she'd tried thanking God for the pain in her hands and that the pain had stopped and hadn't come back.

Someone said to me, "Isn't it hypocritical to thank God for something you're not really thankful for?" I could only answer that the strange thing is that you begin to feel thankful as you say the words of thanksgiving. I think of the old cistern with the pump. You had to prime the pump and pour in some water while furiously pumping the handle before the water would start to come up from the depths. Now it wasn't hypocritical to pour in the water and pump the handle, it was just what you had to do in order to get the water started. It's the same way with praise and thanksgiving; they prime the pump so that the Living Water, the power of God can flow.

I wish you and I had the opportunity to sit down and talk together for a while so I could know just where you're hurting, but it really isn't important for me to know, is it? I couldn't do anything about it anyway. Only God can, and he's eager to help you.

You may think you're married to the wrong man or woman, or you may hate your job, or your child may be on drugs, or you're depressed, or you're not able to make ends meet financially, or you may fear Satan and what he can do to you, or your mate may have been unfaithful to you and you don't know what to do. Whatever it is, begin to give thanks for it right now, and whenever you think about your situation, give thanks.

As I was writing this chapter I had a phone call from a woman who was distraught. Her husband had asked her for a divorce. What was she to do? I asked her if she could trust the goodness of God, whatever it was—whether it was the breakup of her marriage or its mending—and she said she could. "Then let's thank him for the mess you're in right now." We thanked God for her husband just as he was. I reminded her to thank God often, and she said she would. Several days later, she called and sounded jubilant. She said she had never seen such positive results so quickly before in her life. Then she brought up another problem, and I said, "You're to thank God for that, too." "Of course," she said, "I will."

There's nothing that comes into your life that God can't and won't use for good. Stop playing "Why should it happen to me?" Just begin thanking God.

Loving Father, right now I want to thank and praise you for this situation (and tell him about it). I'm going to continue to thank and praise you for it. Thank you, Father, thank you, thank you, thank you . . .

DO IT TO THESE MY BROTHERS

As we grow on a diet of meat and milk we eventually move out of the game of "selfishness" and are strong enough to begin doing helpful things for others. As our own relationship with the Father and the Son grows, we long to share our love with others in tangible ways. As we move into the maturity of sonship and daughtership, the empowering of the Holy Spirit thrusts us into the world of need at our doorstep, in our nation, and beyond.

There's a portion of scripture that I think we need to read to see what it says to us, Matthew 25:34–26:1. It deals with our relationship with those who are hungry and thirsty, the naked and sick, those in prison, and those who are strangers.

I know it's important to come into a deep personal relationship with Jesus and to nurture it in many different ways—such as spending time reading the Bible and devotionals, meeting in prayer groups and in churches for praise and worship, attending conferences, retreats, and talks where faith can be stirred. But there's danger that all our time will be spent in letting the life and love of Jesus pour into us to make us feel good without letting it pour out in active service to others.

In order to have a balanced life we need time spent in withdrawal for renewal and time spent involved in helping others.

Meditation and prayer are essential for growth into spiritual maturity. They bring us into a oneness with God. They help us get it all together, and they enable us to get instructions as to what we are to do for whom and how to do it.

I think of Dr. George Washington Carver who tuned in daily to hear the Lord, whom he referred to as "Mr. Creator." Dr. Carver, like many of us, wanted God to reveal vast secrets to him from his universe, but he finally settled on learning about the peanut. Listening morning after morning, God used him to unlock the secrets of the lowly peanut to find scores of products to make from it; and the economy of the South was revolutionized.

God will speak to us to show us how he'll use

us in our world today, if we'll take the time to listen. Most of us want to stop short of a full relationship with God because we've gotten hung-up on one or more little side roads or games such as speaking in tongues or spiritualism (or a dozen other things).

Most of us have enjoyed the wooing, the courtship, and the honeymoon of Christian experience, but we've put off the business of getting down to the nitty-gritty of life that daily demands anything and everything of us.

A group of women in my church have been compelled by the love of Jesus to serve others. They weren't content to stay at the honeymoon stage; they've moved into mature love. They learned about new mothers at the county hospital who took their babies home wrapped in newspapers, and they began to make simple layettes for the babies. Oh, yes, they give through the outreach of our church on the local, national, and world level, but they saw Jesus naked in those babies, and they clothed him and are continuing to clothe him. They're ever alert to hear the voice of Jesus saying, "Take care of my sheep." They've refused to take the easy way of staying isolated and ingrown and have moved out to do helpful, loving things for the brothers of Jesus.

Jesus had a way of upsetting the religious people of his day—those who thought themselves righteous, who lived according to the law, who'd become isolated and ingrown and who played their little pious games. Rather than going to every religious meeting he could, he spent time with tax collectors, whores, gluttons, drunks—the very people the pious game-players would have nothing to do with. He conversed with a woman at a well, an unheard of thing for a good man to do, and she was from a group of people the game-players shunned. In fact, they went miles out of their way in order to avoid going through their land and having any contact with them.

He failed to obey the game-players who said you can't work on the sabbath. He healed a man on that sacred day. He also harvested enough grain for him and his disciples from a field. He often did the unexpected. Instead of mourning with those who mourned the dead, he restored the dead to life. Instead of eating with the game-players, he called a hated tax collector to come down out of a tree and take him home for lunch. Instead of making a woman, and a bad woman at that, sell some precious oil and give the money to help the poor, he allowed her to anoint his feet. He healed the servant of a man who wasn't only of another race, a Roman, but who was also a pagan. He talked with a couple of men who had been dead for many years. He expanded the idea of a neighbor from the person next door to anyone who needed help. He equated himself with those who were sick, in prison, hungry, thirsty, lonely, and naked, and said that if we did good to any of them it was the same as doing it for him. He taught through his own life that a life of devotion and prayer and love issued forth in a life of action in a world of need. His final words to Peter were about taking care of and feeding his sheep.

He has words for each one of us. He has something for each of us to do in his world. He calls us to faith and to works. Have you heard him speak to you through the book of James, that wonderful handbook for action? I don't know what he would have you do, only he can tell you. But there is one thing I can tell you: it's very likely that right where you are, with the very people in your family and at your place of work, in your church and service organizations, there are needs he wants to meet through you.

Years ago Glenn Clark, a Spirit-led man, invited me to his room to pray with him. When I arrived, he welcomed me and let me in. He walked to a little straight-backed chair and sat down on it and motioned me to kneel in front of him. Then he took a long, narrow, yellow grosgrain ribbon from his pocket, and he crossed my wrists and bound them with the ribbon. He prayed that Jesus would accept me as a slave girl and take me anywhere in the world at anytime to do anything. I've been many places since that time, and there have been times that he's said, "Stay where you are. Right there with those people is where I want you." I've tried to listen and obey. He's teaching me that in helping others near or far, I'm doing for him. And you know, there are times when I think I hear him say with great love and tenderness, "Jo, do it to these my brothers. Take care of my sheep."

Loving Father, I want to leave behind all pious games. I want to stop playing them right now. I don't want any games or hang-ups that would keep me from the maturity you've called me to in Christ Jesus. May my roots go down deep in him, and may I be grounded in him so that I may take my life from him, going or staying as he would have me, living honestly, creatively, and helpfully, bearing much fruit. Amen and Amen.

SUGGESTIONS FOR ADDITIONAL READING

Bach, George R., and Wyden, Peter. *The Intimate Enemy*. New York: William Morrow & Co., 1968.

Carothers, Merlin R. *Power in Praise*. Plainfield, N.J.: Logos International, 1972.

Clark, Glenn. *How to Find Health Through Prayer*. New York: Harper & Brothers, 1940.

Jung, C. G. *Memories, Dreams, Reflections*. New York: Random House, 1961.

Karlins, Marvin, and Andrews, Lewis M. *Biofeedback*. Philadelphia: J. B. Lippincott Co., 1972.

Kimmel, Jo. *Steps to Prayer Power*. Nashville: Abingdon Press, 1972.

Laubach, Frank. *You Are My Friends*. New York: Harper & Brothers, 1942.

Maltz, Maxwell. *Psycho-cybernetics*. New York: Prentice-Hall, 1960.

Maslow, Abraham H. *Toward a Psychology of Being*. Princeton, N.J.: D. Van Nostrand, 1962.

Murray, Andrew. *Abide in Christ*. New York: Grosset & Dunlap, 1968.

Neal, Emily Gardiner. *The Healing Power of Christ*. New York: Hawthorn Books, 1972.

Parkhurst, Genevieve. *Healing and Wholeness Are Yours*. St. Paul, Minn.: Macalester Park, 1957.

Sanford, Agnes. *Let's Believe*. New York: Harper & Brothers, 1954.

Sanford, John. *The Kingdom Within*. Philadelphia: J. B. Lippincott Co., 1970.

Shostrom, Everett L. *Man, the Manipulator*. Nashville: Abingdon Press, 1967.

Steadman, Alice A. *Who's the Matter with Me*. Lakemont, Ga.: CSA Press, 1972.

Vincent, Howell S. *Lighted Passage*. Los Angeles: New Age Publishing Co., n.d.

Weatherhead, Leslie. *The Transforming Friendship*. Nashville: Abingdon-Cokesbury Press, n.d.

Wilson, Kenneth L. *Angel at Her Shoulder*. New York: Harper & Row, 1964.